George McHenry

A Paper Containing a Statement of Facts Relating to the Approaching Cotton Crisis

Vol. 1

George McHenry

A Paper Containing a Statement of Facts Relating to the Approaching Cotton Crisis
Vol. 1

ISBN/EAN: 9783337379339

Printed in Europe, USA, Canada, Australia, Japan

Cover: Foto ©ninafisch / pixelio.de

More available books at **www.hansebooks.com**

A PAPER

CONTAINING A

STATEMENT OF FACTS

RELATING TO THE

APPROACHING COTTON CRISIS.

BY GEORGE McHENRY

RICHMOND, DEC. 31, 1864.

HOUSE OF REPRESENTATIVES,
RICHMOND, January 6, 1865.

SIR:

I herewith enclose copy of a resolution adopted by the Committee of Ways and Means yesterday, asking the favor of you to furnish, at such time and in such form as may be most convenient to yourself, the information sought by the resolution.

I am, very respectfully,
Your obedient servant,

F. S. LYON, *Ch'n.*

GEORGE McHENRY, ESQ.

Resolved, That the Chairman of the Committee of Ways and Means be instructed to address a letter to Mr McHenry, and request him to furnish such information and statistics on the cotton products and cotton trade, and its importance to the commerce of the world, as may be in his possession, and in such form as will be best suited to bring the information easily and prominently before the public.

Office of the Committee of Ways and Means, House of Representatives, January 5, 1865: Resolution, of which the foregoing is a copy, adopted.

F. S. LYON, *Ch'n.*

CORNER 7TH AND GRACE STS.
Richmond, January 8, 1865.

SIR:

I have to acknowledge the receipt of your communication of the 6th instant, enclosing a copy of a resolution passed by the Committee of Ways and Means, requesting me " to furnish such information and statistics on the cotton products and cotton trade, and its importance to the commerce of the world," as may be in my possession.

In compliance with this request, I herewith send you " a paper containing a statement of facts relating to the approaching Cotton Crisis," and shall be happy to furnish any additional information in my possession that may be desired.

I have the honor to be,
Very respectfully,
Your obedient servant,

GEO. McHENRY.

HON. F. S LYON,
Ch'n Com. Ways and Means, House Rep's.

THE COTTON CRISIS.

A pretty general belief exists in the minds of people on both sides of the Atlantic, that the "cotton famine" is over, and that the inhabitants of the globe have, in a great measure, by reason of an increased production in other countries, become independent of the Southern States for a supply of that raw material. This paper is intended to demonstrate that such views are incorrect; that as yet there has been no actual "cotton famine;" that that calamity is still in store, unless the war in America should cease before long, and that the production in "other countries" has not, to any great extent, been augmented. The writer was one of the few Americans, who, at the time of the fall of Fort Sumter, held to the idea that cotton was not *then* king; and he now finds himself almost alone in asserting the political power of the leading article of commerce, provided the rulers of the Confederate States think proper to take steps by which the mercantile monarch may be reinstated upon his throne.

The annexed tables A, B, C, D, E, F, G and H, compiled chiefly from the Board of Trade returns, show the course of the British cotton trade for the last six years. The period begins at the cessation of the commercial panic of 1857—when overproduction commenced—and ends with the close of last year: thus furnishing, at a glance, the history of the cotton imports, exports, stocks, manufactures and sales for home consumption in England, Wales, Scotland and Ireland, for the three seasons anterior, and the three seasons subsequent to the secession of the Southern States from the Federal Union; and, likewise, exhibiting the *increase* in the stocks of cotton and cotton goods during the first division, and the *decrease* during the second division of that time. In analyzing the tables, reference will be made to the present position of the cotton trade.

The largest importations of raw cotton into England took place in 1860, when 1,390,938,752 pounds were imported, at a cost of £35,756,889; and the smallest receipts were in 1862, when but 523,973,296 pounds were imported, valued at £31,093,045. The quantity in 1861 was 1,256,984,736 pounds, worth £38,653,398; and in 1863 it was 669,583,264 pounds, worth £56,277,953.

The exportations of raw cotton in 1860, were 250,428,640 pounds, valued at £5,388,190; for 1861, 298,287,920 pounds, valued at £8,577,747; for 1862, 214,714,528 pounds, valued at £13,508,631; and for 1863, 241,570,992 pounds, valued at £20,145,911—the exportations in comparison with the importations being very great the two latter years.

The yarn-producing capacity, or net weight of the cotton, after spinning, that remained in the United Kingdom for manufacturing purposes, was in 1860, 969,433,595 pounds; and in 1863, only 285,221,515 pounds—showing the fact of the extra loss in working the inferior sorts, and accounting for the additional quantity of cotton required to make a yard of goods in 1863 over what was needed for that purpose in 1860.

Although the cost of the imports of raw cotton into Great Britain, notwithstanding the smaller quantity, was so much greater in 1863 than in 1860, the value of the exports, not much diminished in quantity, was also augmented—making the net cost for that material in 1860, £30,368,699, and in 1863, £36,132,037. And it has been estimated that the profits on the old stocks of cotton goods held over in foreign markets, belonging to English merchants, and disposed of in 1863, amounted to £16,000,000—thereby reducing the exchanges to about £20,000,000, or £10,000,000 less than in 1860. As the old stocks are now about exhausted, that means of payment will cease, and, of course, a greater sum of money will be required, in future, to settle for the cotton supplies of Great Britain.

The largest exportations of cotton piece goods were in 1860, when 2,776,218,427 yards were shipped, along with 197,343,655 pounds of twist and yarn—the value of the clearances footing up, including hosiery and small wares, £52,012,380. Except for hosiery, &c., the figures for 1862 were smaller than in any other year. The total exports reached in value £36,750,971. The quantity that year comprised 1,681,394,600 yards of cloth, 93,225,890 pounds of twist and yarn, and £1,986,265 worth of hosiery, &c. In 1863, 1,706,572,858 yards of piece goods, and 74,642,146 pounds of twist and yarn were sent abroad, valued, with hosiery and small wares, at £47,443,964. The exportations of British cotton goods in the last eight months of 1861, and during the whole of the year 1862, were, with trifling exceptions, purely speculative transactions. There was no foreign demand for British fabrics; and it was to prevent losses at home that shipments were made abroad and advances in money obtained thereon, in the hope that a continued dearth of raw cotton would eventually enhance the value of cotton goods. It was many months before the quotations for manufactured goods responded to the price of the raw material, which had been forced up by speculation, predicated on the continuance of the war, and not by any real demand from the spinners. In fact, the raw material, through the influence of that speculation, had risen so much in value at Liverpool, that the stocks of cotton that were purchased and held at many of the continental ports for the purpose of manufacture, were attracted to England. The advances made on shipments of merchandise to foreign countries and the Possessions of Great Britain are facilities afforded by one class of British merchants to another class.

There has been a very slight reduction in the British home consumption of cotton manufactures. The prices of cotton goods have not risen in the same ratio with the advance in raw cotton, from the fact of the raw material not amounting, in ordinary times, to more than 30 per cent. of the value of the manufactured article, at manufacturers' prices. But now that cotton forms the principal cost of the fabric—about 65 per cent.—the prices of goods will advance proportionately higher, as the markets for the staple ascend. The decrease in consumption has indeed been so small, that it does not amount to any thing of moment: it is doubtful whether, even if more than the natural yearly increase in the consumption has been checked. The rich purchase nearly as freely as ever; the poor never, even in the most prosperous times, bought more than sufficient for their own wants, and their wants were always moderate. This is clearly demonstrated by the quantity of cotton goods imported into England from other countries. The receipts from abroad in 1863 were about the same as in 1860. The value, however, was augmented from £758,030 in 1860, to £1,034,904 in 1863. While British cotton goods contained, as just stated, on the average, at normal prices, about 30 per cent. of value in raw cotton, Continental and Eastern cotton goods possessed less value in raw material—their cost principally, or to a much greater degree, originating from the additional labor and the design—none but the fancy and the finest description of cotton goods are imported into the British Isles.

In 1860, £1,000 sterling's worth of British cotton goods, at manufacturers' prices, contained raw cotton to a value of £300. In 1863, the same weight and kind of goods contained raw cotton, allow ng for the extra loss in spinning inferior cotton, to the value of £1,200 sterling: thus causing an increase in cost of £900—making what stood £1,000 in 1860, come up to £1,900 in 1863. Yet, while the "middle men" and the retailers have been contented with a less per centage of profit than formerly, the manufacturers received more than two prices. And those manufacturers complain, unjustly, that they do not receive a proper equivalent for their goods. Their plausible complaints have been listened to by the masses, for it is known, that while cotton was selling at four prices, the actual consumer was only paying about double the old rates for inferior goods. The community, generally, supposed the manufacturers to have been great sufferers by the so-called "cotton famine." They have, on the contrary, been great gainers by the partial stoppage of supplies. In addition to their usual emolument, they have had, and are now having the advantage of gradually rising markets for their goods. The cotton spinners and cotton manufacturers have been pretty much in the condition of the proprietors of flour mills after a bad harvest; for those millers then obtain constantly advancing prices for their flour: every bushel of wheat which they purchase yields more profit than when the crops have been large, because the quotations of grain affect those for flour, and the time consumed in the manufacture affords an opportunity for an advance in the markets. In fact, the cotton manufacturer has an advantage over the flour mill owner, for the reason that it takes longer to convert raw cotton into cloth than wheat into flour.

The sterling figures given for the exportation of cotton manufactures, are the declared value at the custom house. Those values are no doubt incorrect—the goods, probably, are under-invoiced at least

33½ per cent., in order to evade a portion of the duties levied upon their importation at the ports to which they were destined. Nearly all, if not all of the importing countries place *ad valorem* duties upon cotton goods. A near approximation to the value of the British exports of cotton manufactures will, therefore, be arrived at by adding 50 per cent. to the given figures. It must, too, be borne in mind that there are many articles of British wool, flax and silk manufacture, that contain a mixture of cotton, which are not included in this statement. So, the cotton trade of England is more extended than appearances would indicate.

The stocks of cotton and yarns and goods in the hands of all classes in the United Kingdom, when reduced to the weight of raw cotton—its yarn-producing capacity—were as follows:

DATE.	Raw Cotton in Warehouse.	Raw Cotton in Spinners' Hands.	Yarns and Goods on Hand	TOTAL.
Jan. 1, 1858, -	155,007,301 lbs.	85,900,000 lbs.	400,000,000 lbs.	640,907,301 lbs.
Jan. 1, 1859, -	96,865,677 "	95,000,000 "	415,000,000 "	606,865,677 "
Jan. 1, 1860, -	168,014,154 "	105,000,000 "	465,000,000 "	738,014,154 "
Jan. 1, 1861, -	206,486,450 "	135,000,000 "	510,000,000 ".	851,486,450 "
Jan. 1, 1862, -	218,755,837 "	80,000,000 "	460,000,000 "	758,755,837 "
Jan. 1, 1863, -	107,041,247 "	35,000,000 "	270,000,000 "	412,041,871 "
Jan. 1, 1864, -	74,186,871 "	15,000,000 "	100,000,000 "	189,186,871 "

When the trade is in its usual state of vigor, the stocks of raw cotton in the warehouses and in spinners' hands, are not at their highest point on New Year's day. The largest stocks of raw cotton *in warehouse* were at the following dates:

1844, July	12,	-	-	998,405	bales.
1845, August	1,	-	-	1,057,375	"
1846, January	16,	-	-	894,838	"
1847, April	20,	·	-	539,719	"
1848, June	30,	-	-	657,750	"
1849, July	6,	-	-	752,480	"
1850, April	12,	-	-	571,166	"
1851, July	18,	-	-	735,497	"
1852, July	23,	-	-	694,794	"
1853, July	15,	-	-	879,650	"
1854, July	21,	-	-	970,107	"
1855, April	20,	-	-	666,658	"
1856, August	15,	-	-	813,266	"
1857, May	29,	-	-	693,509	"
1858, June	11,	-	-	678,636	"
1859, June	24,	-	-	754,109	"
1860, April	24,	-	-	1,015,868	"

The particulars of the largest stocks in warehouse at the ports since 1860 are not at hand. The *bales*, subsequent to 1861, have been so irregular in weight, and the cotton itself so varied in quality, that the quantity, when stated by bales, would not indicate the true condition of the trade. The greater part of the American crops arrive in Europe between December and May.

The expense for cotton clothing to the inhabitants of the United Kingdom of Great Britain and Ireland was as follows:

In 1858,	-	-	-	- £ 23,000,000
In 1859,	-	-	-	- 23,500,000
In 1860,	-	-	-	- 25,000,000
In 1861,	-	-	-	- 28,000,000
In 1862,	-	-	-	- 33,000,000
In 1863,	-	-	-	- 44,000,000
In 1864,	-	-	-	- 60,000,000

These amounts are at manufacturers' prices. From the fact of there having been something over three years' supply on hand when the American conflict began, the British people, as a community, have not felt the pressure of the increased cost for their cotton fabrics to any great extent. But now that the cottons purchased at low cost have all been consumed, and four or five prices have to be paid, for every pound required, the drain upon the resources of the English people for that description of clothing will be very serious, and greatly derange their financial concerns. It makes no difference what they pay for their raw cotton which is re-exported in the raw or in the manufactured state. It is only through the enhanced cost of the quantity consumed at home that they will suffer greatly ; for, on all that which is re-exported, no matter in what condition, there is a corresponding advance in price. The cost for the raw cotton contained in the home-consumed cotton goods in 1860, was about £7,500,000. In 1865, it will be, at the lowest calculation, £42,-500,000, or a difference of £35,000,000. That large sum is not seen in the government returns, because no account of what is consumed by the people is ever taken ; but it must necessarily soon begin to be felt, if it has not already done so, in the money market. That increase in the cost for raw cotton in 1865, over the figures of 1860, will be equal to four times the amount of the income tax, to one-third more than the interest on the national debt, and fully one-half of the yearly outlay of the British government. Unlike the annual expenditure of the British nation, however, the whole of the sum, will be sent to other places, thereby causing a real drain upon the country to an amount double the cost of all the food imported. An increase in the cost of breadstuffs, after a bad harvest, of only a few million of pounds sterling, creates a disturbance in the money market. What a revulsion must then take place when not only the £35,000,000 additional expense is incurred for the cost of home consumed cotton, but when an extra capital will be requisite for conducting the commerce in cotton with other nations. Nor will this anticipated panic in the money market lower the prices of cottons. No doubt the state of the finances very materially affects the value of cotton, when there are large stocks on hand ; but with light stocks, the rate of discount will produce but little change in the quotations, although interest is an important feature in the cotton trade, from the fact of the raw material being longer in its transit from the planter to the consumer than any other article of commerce.

In the case of a bad harvest, which always creates high rates for money, the value of wheat is not affected by an increase in interest, because wheat is then wanted, and the supply and demand regulate the price : there are no old stocks to draw upon. So it is just now

2

with cotton, and there is no danger of a tightness in money causing a depreciation in its value. Breadstuffs, to be sure, go immediately into consumption, and the loss of interest upon them is very trifling, while it takes months for cotton to reach the actual consumer. But the prospective condition of the cotton market is such that the item of interest need not be considered in determining its price. This is the first time in the history of the world that there has been any thing like an approach to a "raiment famine;" and few persons, therefore, seem to comprehend the difficulty. The hiatus caused by the partial loss of three cotton crops, 1862, 1863 and 1864, in the Southern States of America, must be felt. The quantity cultivated in those states since the second year of the war has not more than compensated for that which has been destroyed in order to prevent its falling into the hands of the enemy, to say nothing of the wastage, and what has been consumed within the limits of the Confederacy. If the application of the torch has been suspended, the consumption and wastage still go on. There was two years' supply of cotton and cotton goods in every shape at the consuming points in 1858; in 1860–61, enough for three years in all parts of the world—the increased production of southern cotton in 1858, 1859 and 1860, having given an additional year's requirements. The quantity of cotton in the whole world, with cotton goods, is less by 8,500,000 bales than it was four years ago. High prices have reduced the stocks of cotton and cotton goods, but they have not stimulated production to any great degree in other countries, because the labor could not be much diverted from the accustomed pursuits of their inhabitants. Only a few months' extra consumption has been cultivated, under the influence of extravagant quotations. A careful calculation, made a short time since, shows that the increase in the quantity of cotton grown in all countries other than the Southern States, in 1864 over 1860, was only equal to 350,000 bales of American in weight. The augmented receipts from those other countries was owing chiefly to the drain upon old stocks. The Southern States have, since the establishment of the blockade, contributed to the "outer world" about 900,000 bales of cotton—part of which has been exported through the blockade, and part stolen by the Yankees. So, with the stocks on hand, the supplies from other quarters, and the cotton that has escaped from the Confederacy, the "famine" has, up to the present time, been tided over.

Formerly, the number of *bales* of American cotton manufactured in Great Britain amounted to 85 per cent. of the entire quantity, counting by bales, taken by the mills. But the American bales were heavier than those of other countries, and the cotton produced more yarn to the pound than that grown elsewhere. British fabrics then, it will be found, have hitherto actually contained 90 per cent. of American cotton. The case is now reversed; and it is probable that the cotton goods manufactured last year, and being made this year, • do not contain more than 20 per cent. of American cotton. In order to work the inferior sorts, and to augment the weight of the fabrics, a large admixture of mineral and other substances was, and is being used. This is considered a fraud, as most of the sales are negotiated with the understanding that the goods contain the usual proportion of American cotton. No description of merchandise, as before remarked, is so long reaching the consumer from the producer as cotton goods; and the complaints in reference to the inferiority of the texture of the articles have been slow in coming to hand. Now, however, that the deception is being discovered. British cotton fabrics are losing their reputation. Shoddy cotton cloth will not answer the wants of the world. East India and other inferior cottons, unless in very small proportions, are unfit for machine made goods. They may look nearly as well when overloaded with "size," but they certainly will not wear so long. The following extract from the *Friend of India* of June 9, 1864, a newspaper published at Calcutta, will no doubt be perused with interest, as it shows the condition in which British cotton goods arrive at the places of consumption. Even the ladies of England are now complaining that their stockings and other cotton garments "last no time at all:"

MILDEW IN CLOTH.

(Extract from the Friend of India, June 9, 1864.)

Ever since Manchester became dependent upon India for her working material, her manufactures have, to the surprise of no one, fallen off very materially in quality. If there has been any surprise in the matter, it is that even Manchester ingenuity should have succeeded in turning out cloth, composed entirely of Indian cotton, to bear so favorable a comparison with the old makes as the production of the last two years undoubtedly presents. Any one may recollect how it was at first asserted that no cloth of even decent appearance could be manufactured of Surat cotton, and how, by great labor, and thought, and expense, the machinery of Lancashire has been so modified and reconstructed that not only the best Surats, but even common Bengal, has been brought into good use. And when the first instalments of the new cotton cloth were received here, importers were very agreeably astonished to find that it should be of so very saleable a description; and the native dealers exhibited, in many instances, a preference to the new cloth over the old. This opinion is now reversed. The new cloth is taken because there is no other to be had, but it is taken with great suspicion. It is all intrinsically rotten. All of it contain the seed of unsoundness, which, if left to itself, germinates in due time into rottenness. With the best information in our possession, we have no hesitation in asserting that one-third of that class of imports known as "gray goods" is landed here more or less damaged by mildew. The very samples received in tin cases by the quick route overland are black with mildew. The goods arrive here sometimes partially rotten, so that when the bales are opened patches of the cloth attach to the packing paper, and crumble to dust when handled. Some bales are turned along the edges of the cloth like very mouldy cheese; some are covered with small black spots which have wormed themselves into the very heart of the bale; while others open out in apparently good condition—sufficient evidence, however, of the latent unsoundness being afforded by the mouldy smell and the hot damp feel of the cloth. Of the number of damaged bales resold by the importers, and otherwise privately arranged for, we can scarcely venture to offer an estimate. But so notorious has the evil become that in some quarters it has been found advisable to accept as an established conclusion that all gray goods are more or less damaged, and to regulate transactions upon that basis, the importer surrendering a certain proportion of the market value of sound goods, and the native dealer accepting the risks of damage to the goods, however serious the damage may prove.

There is now a very decided opinion here, and we understand the same view is entertained in other places, as to the cause of this mildew damage. When it was first discovered, and the cases of damage were less frequent and less serious, it was attributed to external influences during transit, or to long storage of the goods in damp godowns in India. As instances multiplied, however, it came to be a general opinion that the mildew was contracted in the packers' warehouses at home; and many attempts were made to claim upon the packers for the losses sustained in foreign markets, all which attempts proved ineffectual. It now appears to be an ascertained fact that the damage arises from the injurious nature of the ingredients used in preparing the "size"—that is, the liquid composition employed to stiffen the warps before weaving. It is noticed, too, that in the cloths now arriving here is an unusual quantity of this "sizing," and it has been ascertained that this extra quantity is used for the purpose of obtaining an increase of weight, cloth being sold by weight. In on* of those home cotton circulars whose usefulness we have previously had occasion to acknowledge, the cloth now being manufactured is described as "compounded in a great measure of paste and refuse," and the same circular goes to say that "consumers every where are getting disgusted at the inferior quality of the fabrics made out of short-stapled cotton." But although it is acknowledged that the damage originates with the manufacturer, it has not yet been found practicable to substantiate a claim against him for compensation to the buyer. Indian merchants pay dearer than ever for the goods they import into this country, and although these goods prove unsaleable, or saleable only at a heavy sacrifice, the loss is all borne here

Many of the Lancashire mills had their machinery altered to suit the spinning of Indian cotton. It is discovered, however, that that very alteration is likewise beneficial to the spinning of American cotton. The great difficulty to which the mill owners will be subjected, after the trade resumes its former extent, will be the absence of the requisite number of operatives. Many of the operatives have lost their skill by being engaged in other employments. Paving streets and breaking stone physically incapacitates them for manufacturing cotton. Others have emigrated, and the ranks of the operatives, which have been further thinned by disease and death, have not been recruited by the usual fresh accessions in the last four years.

Cotton is grown in about sixty different countries; but the Confederate States present the only instance where it is cultivated as a leading crop. The following were the imports into Great Britain in 1863:

Russia—Growth of Khiva and Bokhara,	632	cwts.
Portugal,	6,105	"
Spain—Ports without the Mediterranean,	91	"
Ports within the Mediterranean,	1,140	"
Canary Islands,	3	"
Italy—Genoa,	284	"
Naples,	2,396	"
Sicily,	1,875	"
Venetia,	228	"
Illyria, Croatia and Dalmatia,	576	"
Malta,	3,400	"
Greece,	3,080	"
European Turkey,	12,180	"
Natolia or Asia Minor,	96,696	"
Syria and Palestine,	1,418	"
Egypt,	835,289	"
Africa—British Possessions on river Gambia,	131	"
Sierra Leone,	24	"
British Possessions on the Gold coast,	95	"
West coast of Africa,	659	"
Cape of Good Hope,	33,845	"
Natal,	237	"
Mauritius,	1,609	"
British India—Bombay,	3,004,196	"
Madras,	441,582	"
Bengal,	397,864	"
Singapore,	1,952	"
Ceylon,	33,163	"
French Possessions in India,	515	"
Phillippine Islands,	155	"
Siam,	1	"
China (exclusive of Hong Kong).	145,134	"
Hong Kong,	130,369	"
Japan,	6,352	"
Australia—Victoria,	13	"
New South Wales,	121	"
Queensland,	122	"
British West India Islands—Jamaica,	1,826	"

	Brought forward,		5,165,158	cwts.
British West India Islands—St. Christopher,		-	20	"
	Antigua,	- -	65	"
	St. Lucia,	- -	11	"
	St. Vincent,	- -	636	"
(South American growth)	Barbadoes,	- -	16.556	"
	Grenada,	- -	1,154	"
	Tobago,	- -	30	"
	Trinidad,	- -	162	"
British Guiana—Demarara,		- -	2,368	"
	Berbice,	- -	1	"
Belize,	- -	- -	3,899	"
Dutch Guiana,	- -	- -	807	"
Foreign West Indies—Porto Rico,		- -	2,553	"
	Curacoa,	- -	170	"
	St. Thomas,	- -	1,338	"
Hayti and the Dominican Republic,		- -	5,931	"
Central America—Ports on the Atlantic,		- -	12	"
	Ports on the Pacific,	- -	335	"
New Grenada—Ports on the Atlantic,		- -	22,683	"
Venezuela,	- -	- -	742	"
Ecuador,	- -	- -	278	"
Peru,	- -	- -	160	"
Brazil,	- -	- -	201,814	"
Uruguay,	- -	- -	22	"
Argentine Confederation,		- -	33	"
				5,427,138 cwts.

Confederate cotton received through the following countries:

Norway,	-	-	-	70 "
Sweden,	-	-	-	252 "
Holland,	-	-	-	1,047 "
Denmark,	-	-	-	165 "
Prussia,	-	-	-	23 "
Hamburgh,	-	-	-	2,941 "
Bremen,	-	-	-	617 "
France,	-	-	-	15,033 "
Belgium,	-	-	-	2,183 "
Channel Islands,	-	-	-	1 "
Canada,	-	-	-	153 "
New Brunswick,	-	-	-	19 "
Nova Scotia and Cape Breton,		-	-	1,828 "
Bermuda,	-	-	-	63,807 "
Bahamas,	-	-	-	202,009 "
Mexico,	-	-	-	172,126 "
Cuba,	-	-	-	31,920 "
United States,	-	-	-	47,117 "
Confederate States, *direct*,		-	-	9,973 "
				551,284 cwts.

Total imports,   5,978,422 cwts.

It will be observed that most of the producing countries furnish but little cotton, and there is no likelihood whatever of their being able to increase their yield. *They have not the labor to do so.* The high prices at Liverpool, it will be seen by the above statement, have attracted to the United Kingdom a portion of the old stocks of American cotton that were at the continental ports.

India has never produced in any one year as much as 2,000,000 bales; which, considering her enormous population, is a very small quantity. Her people in fact have difficulty in raising enough food for their own wants. For the six years ending December 31, 1863, India took as much cotton in the shape of yarns and goods as she exported to all countries of that material in its raw state. She usually takes more cotton in goods from, than she sends of raw cotton to England. It has been only by exporting her old stocks of cotton that she has been enabled to balance her imports with her exports within the period named. India, too, does not buy her own cottons back again in the manufactured condition, but requires to be furnished with cotton fabrics made from good American cottons. A large portion of the imports of India cotton is re-exported from England to the Continent of Europe. There is no change of fashion in India, and her people, therefore, want cotton goods that will wear for a regular length of time. The subjoined statement of the commerce of India in cotton, cotton yarns and cotton goods, outward and inward, confirms the assertion just made:

Receipts of Raw Cotton from India, and Yarns and Goods exported thereto from the United Kingdom, with estimates of the Indian Commerce in Cotton and Cotton Goods with other countries.

	Gross pounds of raw cotton.	Yarn-producing properties.	Weight of goods and yarns exported to India.
1858, - - -	132 722 576	96 887 481	223 000 000
1859, - - -	192 330 880	138 478 234	305 000 000
1860, - - -	204 141 168	146 981 641	242 000 000
1861, - - -	369 040 448	269 709 123	225 000 000
1862, - - -	392 654 528	270 931 625	145 000 000
1863, - - -	434 420 784	284 729 175	155 000 000
	1 725 310 384	1 207 717 279	1 295 000 000
Add net weight of raw cotton shipped from India to China and other countries, as well as weight of piece goods exported from India, from 1858 to 1863, -		130 000 000	
Yarns and goods shipped from other countries to India, about - - - -		-	42 717 279
Lbs.		1 337 717 279	1 337 717 279

The above figures make no allowance for the stock of raw cotton that was on hand in India on January 1, 1858. As already observed, she could not have contributed the increased quantity to England, if it had not been for those old stocks.

It is quite clear that India has not for a number of years past grown more than enough for her own supply. She has only been enabled to make exportations of cotton, from the fact of receiving such large quantities of cotton yarns and cotton goods from Great Britain; which yarns and goods were made, as before remarked, from better cotton than she parted with. The loss in spinning Surat cotton is set down at 27 per cent. for 1858; 28 per cent. for 1859, 1860 and 1861; 31 per cent. for 1862; and 33½ per cent. for 1863. No Surat cotton can be worked without a loss of 25 per cent.; and every year there has been a considerable quantity imported entirely worthless for manufacturing purposes, which increases the average loss to above that rate. This was the case to a much greater degree in 1862 and 1863 than in previous years, in consequence of the "sweepings" of the old stocks from the interior, as well as cotton that had been used for stuffing furniture and household purposes, having constituted a portion of the importations into England. The average loss in the weight of India cotton, when converted into yarn, for the last six years, was just 30 per cent. The immense increase in the exports of yarns and goods to India in 1859 over 1858, was owing to the demand for British manufactures, which arose after the mutiny was suppressed. The heavy supplies of machine made goods thus attracted thither displaced the old fashioned hand made fabrics, and enabled the Hindoos to release a greater portion of their raw cotton than usual, which accounts for the large receipts from thence in 1861. These large quantities were set in motion before the war was thought of: and the high prices that have since prevailed have resulted in draining the interior, the cultivation not having been much augmented. Although during the first part of the present year (1864) the importations from India were in excess of those at the same period in 1863, it is not believed that the receipts for the whole twelve months will show any increase over last year. The shipments of cotton from India have, for the last four or five months, been losing money—as much as 10d. sterling per lb.—and many firms. who had made large fortunes by the rise in prices, have not only lost all their capital and earnings, but have become bankrupt.

The delusion in reference to the yield of cotton in India—which is now being dispelled—arose from the fact of her "fine" cottons having been celebrated from her earliest history; also, from the fact of her having at one time supplied the whole world with cotton goods. But then, it must be borne in mind, that her production of fine cottons was very limited, and confined altogether to a small district of country, while her growth of coarser cottons, although larger. was insignificant, in comparison with our present ideas of cotton crops. At the period when India supplied the world with cotton goods, the quantity worn of that description of goods was very trifling—wool and flax then constituting the chief materials for clothing. Mexico holds, in respect to cotton, almost an identical position with India ; for, as far back as her history is known, she has been a cotton producing and a cotton manufacturing country. Her cotton fabrics. as recorded by her discoverers, rivaled in quality the long famed goods of India. Indeed, so valuable were they, that small pieces of exquisitely fine cotton cloth were used by the Mexicans for currency. Yet no one has ever attempted to claim for Mexico the position of a large grower of cotton !

China has not for the last half century grown enough cotton for her own wants. Up to 1861 she had. for a number of years, imported about 200,000 bales of cotton from India. She also imports cotton from Burmah, overland by pony caravans: And, likewise, draws large supplies of cotton goods and cotton yarns from England, and cotton goods from the American States. Yet China has not only. for the time being, ceased to be an importer from India, but has actually become an exporter of cotton to England. This change in the course of trade has been accomplished in consequence of the high prices having induced the Chinese to part with their usual stocks;

and India has thus been enabled to send to England what she formerly furnished to China. China and India, being manufacturing as well as producing countries, had, like England, at all times a large supply of the raw material. They have been so drained of cotton, that prices were at last accounts much higher at their markets than at Liverpool.

Egypt is the only country that has made a rapid stride in the production of cotton; and that has been done at the expense of other agricultural pursuits. She has, however, attained her maximum yield—her largest crop being only a little in excess of 300,000 bales.

In the first part of this paper a statement is given of the stocks of cotton and cotton goods within the United Kingdom, at the several annual periods from 1858 to 1864. Large as was the falling off in the stocks of raw cotton last New year's day, the reduction in the stocks of goods was, it will be seen, much greater. In all the discussions that have taken place in England in reference to the cotton supply, the latter, and in reality, most important branch of the question has been entirely overlooked. That omission will soon be made apparent to every one by the force of circumstances; that is, when the shopkeepers of the United Kingdom begin to replenish their stocks in order to meet the demand from their customers; and when the distant consuming countries call for increased supplies, their importations of cotton goods the past two years not having been equal to what they consumed—their old stocks of goods, as long as they lasted, "helped out" the deficiency.

The total exportations of yarns and goods in *weight* from Great Britain, were as follow:

In 1858,	-	-	-	610,741,000 pounds.
In 1859,	-	-	-	633,871,000 "
In 1860,	-	-	-	748,722,000 "
In 1861,	-	-	-	684,886,000 "
In 1862,	-	-	-	410,000,000 "
In 1863,	-	-	-	390,000,000 "
				3,478,220,000 pounds.

These figures present the net weight of the goods. The cotton consumed in producing them increased with the use of the inferior sorts. No doubt, whatever, the exportations of British cotton goods in 1859, 1860 and 1861 were excessive—far beyond what was necessary—and subsequently enabled the Eastern countries to part with more than the usual quantity of their raw cotton; and the high prices ruling since have induced them to export still more of their staple than they otherwise would have consented to release. This fact, coupled with the small receipts of cotton goods from the United Kingdom the past three years, will augment their demand for goods for very many months to come.

The cotton consumed and the cotton yarns and goods produced by the mills of the United Kingdom, were as follows:

DATE.	Cotton Consumed.	Yarns and Goods produced.
1858, · ·	895,600,000 lbs.	795,000,000 lbs.
1859, · ·	966,600,000 "	859,250,000 "
1860, · ·	1,073,600,000 "	973,650,000 "
1861, · ·	997,400,000 "	846,500,000 "
1862, · ·	444,500,000 "	365,000,000 "
1863, · ·	553,260,000 "	460,000,000 "
	4,930,960,000 lbs.	4,230,400,000 lbs.

American cotton loses but 12½ per cent. in the process of conversion into yarn, while other descriptions lose from 20 to 40 per cent.—some even more; in fact, there is great uncertainty as to the yield in yarn, in consequence of the irregularity in quality, and condition of the cotton sent from the eastern countries, as well as South America.

The consumption of cotton by the mills in 1864, has been greater than in either of the two previous years. This, of course, has given additional employment to the operatives. Had it not been, however, for the increased receipts from the Southern States, many of the mills would have been closed. The American cotton coming to hand more freely than was expected, enabled the spinners to consume more of the inferior cottons; and the "cotton famine," was therefore at one time thought by many persons, unfamiliar with the detail of the trade, to be at an end. As already stated, there has been no actual cotton famine. If the American crop of 1861 had reached Liverpool in due course, there would have been no sale for it: the markets were then overstocked with cotton and with cotton goods; and if the war had never taken place, the operatives would have fared just as badly as they have done the past three years—perhaps worse; for, in that event, all the cotton interest of Lancashire must have been ruined by the great depreciation which most assuredly would have taken place. The spinners will not buy raw cotton, unless they have a demand for their goods. The crop of 1861 would, therefore, have remained unsold, except to speculators at very low rates. Some persons are laboring under the mistaken idea that the Confederate Government should have seized that crop, and sent it forward to Europe. It could not have been depended on as a basis of credit; for the moral effect of such a large quantity, even when stored in warehouses at Liverpool, would have had a very depressing influence upon prices. It might have been well, if the Constitution permitted, to have purchased the whole crop of 1861, and kept it within the Confederacy. But it is believed that there is no citizen of any one of the Southern States who in 1861 dreamed that the conflict with the Northern States would have lasted so long. The world was in a condition to do without the planting of 1862. It will be found that it is the loss of the crops of 1863 and 1864 that has influenced prices so greatly. To repeat, it has been a mistake to attribute the distress in the manufacturing districts to a cotton "famine." In 1827, the same sort of distress existed in France. The cotton operatives there were then thrown out of employment, not on account of the absence of the raw material, but in consequence of the overstock of manufactured goods in France, for which there was no demand in other countries. Those overstocks were caused by the erection of too much spinning force in 1825 and 1826. Many of the manufacturers were ruined; and it was not until the year 1831 that the overproduction of goods was consumed, when the cotton mills were set to work again. The importations of cotton into France are principally for her own use. But she, like other manufacturing countries, had, in two seasons, previous to the American troubles, made a large overproduction of cotton goods. She usually consumes within her borders about 80 per cent. of all she imports, or 150,000,000 pounds per annum, being at the rate of 4 pounds per head for her entire population, although many of her inhabitants do not wear any cotton goods. On the other hand, Great Britain, as a general rule, re-exports about 75 per cent. of all she imports, in the raw and in the manufactured state, consuming about 25 per cent. at home. Her people need 9 pounds per head per annum, when the cotton is of good American staple, and of course, a larger quantity when the cotton is of the inferior qualities. The actual home consumption of England in the years named was as follows:

In 1858,	-	-	28 per cent. of the importation.
In 1859,	-	-	25 " "
In 1860,	-	-	23 " "
In 1861,	-	-	29 " "
In 1862,	-	-	90 " "
In 1863,	-	-	75 " "

It is a fortunate thing for England that she was possessed of such large stocks of cotton and cotton goods, when the war broke out, at a cost to her, of 7 pence per pound for the raw material ; and it is also fortunate for her that she has received, directly and indirectly from the Confederacy, since the 1st of September 1863, over 4,000 bales of cotton per week. The English manufacturers and merchants held a stock of cotton and cotton goods, at home and abroad, equal to three years' demand, which they have been dealing out at three, four and five prices. And no sooner did that supply fail, than the Confederacy began to favor them with the much needed staple, at the above named rate per week.

The Yankees, too, have had the benefit of a portion of the exports of Confederate cotton. They have been shipping provisions and clothing to Mexico and the West Indies, and receiving in exchange therefor the southern staple. Had it not been for this course of trade, the federal cotton manufacturers would have been obliged to have continued their importations of the raw material from Europe, and thus have drawn largely upon the scanty stocks on that side of the Atlantic—enhancing the quotations there, and, at the same time, draining the precious metals from the Northern States, as the provisions and clothing shipped by them to Mexico and the Islands would not have found a market elsewhere. Hence, the Yankees would have been obliged to part with their gold. It is a singular coincidence, that no sooner did the large export trade in breadstuffs between the Northern States and Europe, which began just about the time of the secession of the Southern States from the Federal Union, decline to its former limited amount, than these new outlets for Yankee produce were opened up. This, along with sales of clippers and other ships, driven from the seas by the vigilance of Confederate cruisers, and captures, by Yankee men-of-war, of British and Confederate property running the blockade, furnished the federals with supplies, which otherwise must have been bought and paid for in England. King Cotton has, therefore, in this manner, materially assisted the finances of the enemy. On top of all this, the Federals, who have been more successful in finance than the Confederates, have had emissaries in Europe, who have succeeded in placing upon the several stock exchanges, and in various other ways, from £70,000,000 to £100,000,000 of 5-20 bonds.

Quite a brisk trade in cotton has been carried on for some months past, between the Confederate and Federal States, under authority of an act of the Washington Congress, approved July 2, 1864; which reads:

That it shall be lawful for the Secretary of the Treasury, with the approval of the President, to authorize agents to purchase for the United States any productions of the States declared in insurrection, at such places therein as shall be designated by him, at such prices as shall be agreed on by the seller, not exceeding the market value thereof at the place of delivery, nor exceeding three-fourths of the market value thereof in the city of New York at the latest quotation known to the agent purchasing.

While the Yankees have been dealing with the Southern States, under the authority of their Congress, the Confederates have been exchanging produce with them, in violation of the laws of their country. The consequence is, that the North has been getting cheap cotton, and the South has been receiving dear bacon. The trade, on the part of some of the Confederate authorities, has been "winked at." A contraband traffic should not have been permitted. Swapping off a pound of cotton, which should have produced seventy-five cents, according to the above Act of the Federal Congress, for a pound of bacon worth but 20 cents, or thereabouts, in the same currency, was, to say the least of it, very bad business management.

There has been a constant drain of cotton from Arkansas, Louisiana and Texas, through the ports of Galveston and Matamoras, which has been enriching the shoddy men engaged in the transactions, without giving any adequate return to the government or the people of the Confederacy. In many instances where government officials, both civil and military, have had control of cotton, frauds have been practiced to such a shameful degree, that public attention is being drawn to the crime. Blockade running, too, has been conducted at a rate of extravagance never before known. The system inaugurated by the parties having charge of many of the ships engaged in the trade, for costliness, is without a parallel in the history of commerce. There are shoddy captains, shoddy officers, shoddy crews, shoddy engineers, shoddy pilots, shoddy firemen, shoddy stewards, shoddy cooks, etc. etc. The expense of getting a bale of cotton to Liverpool now, is more than the former value of the cotton itself. Very few of the ships bring in full cargoes of supplies; some of them only one-fourth of their capacity, and some nothing at all. All of them, however, take out full cargoes of cotton—even to deck loads. The correspondent of the New York Herald furnishes the following account:

While speaking of this trade, it may not be out of place to allude to the prosperity of Matamoras. Every house is occupied in the city and rents are enormously high. A store which rented for a few hundred dollars only before the cotton trade commenced, now commands thousands of dollars per year. The carpenter and brick mason are busily engaged in erecting stores in every part of the city, and so soon as they are completed they are filled with goods. The expense of living there is from one to three dollars per day in specie. Greenbacks have not been "recognized" by the Emperor yet, and, of course, have to take a back seat. I noticed but little business doing in Brownsville; the terror of our forces being before the eyes of the merchants there, they keep their stocks of goods light. The city of Bagdad also deserves a favorable mention. Where, but three years ago, there were but two or three board shanties, now stands Bagdad a full grown town, with a population of not far from four thousand. It can boast of "first class" hotels, boarding houses, stores well filled with goods, saloons and restaurants without number, and last, though not least, a city police, which maintains order by night and by day. "Cotton is king" in Matamoras and Bagdad, without doubt, for it gives them all the vitality they possess.

It is quite manifest then, that if the Southern States had been in a position to have withheld their cotton from the "outer world," the powers of Europe would by this time have been forced into recognizing their independence. But are not the Confederate States now in a position to retain their cotton? As it is, a large share of the resources of the South have absolutely been dissipated away. Most of the legislation, so far, seems, by its practical operation, to have favored a few speculators, who, so long as they had a "monopoly" of the trade by their contracts, by which they were making 7 or 800 per cent., did not care to see peace brought about. The trade ought to have been open to every one, free from all restrictions, and then the Confederacy would have had a constituency in Europe of sufficient influence to put a pressure upon the governments in favor of recognition. As it is, the trade has, by unwise arrangements, been thrown into the hands of a few individuals, who have neither social nor political influence on the other side of the Atlantic.

It may be well here to remark, that in 1810, Spain, in consideration of England's attempt to mediate in all disputes with the South American Colonies, permitted her to carry on a direct trade with them. In a short time, by that means, the Spanish American republics had a mercantile constituency in England; and it was owing to the influence of that constituency that England eventually recognized the independence of those republics. The Southern States, unfortunately, have no such constituency, to demand justice for them at the doors of the Foreign office in Downing street. Nor is this all: While the exports of the Confederacy (including specie) should have within the past sixteen months netted £25,000,000 sterling, the imports could not have amounted to over one-fifth that sum. In fact, by the system adopted, five bales of cotton have been given away, when one bale would have answered. What is the use of buying ships and purchasing supplies, and paying for the same in cotton at 6d. per pound, when the cotton is really worth 28d. per pound. It is in this manner that the resources of these States are being frittered away. It has been a mistake from first to last, to mix up the supplies for the Confederacy with cotton. Surely, it would be better to pay for all the foreign supplies in gold, and retain the cotton. The gold would buy an amount of supplies five times greater than can be obtained under the present system : and what is more, the gold would go into the bank vaults, and help to lower the rate of discount in Lombard street, and thus put an extra value on cotton, while the cotton goes to Manchester, and assists the manufacturers, as already explained, in staving off the cotton famine. If it be deemed expedient to continue the shipments of cotton, instead of sending forward gold to purchase supplies, it would be well to have the cotton stored in warehouse at Liverpool, and not sold. It is quite as easy to borrow money upon cotton when it is in England, as to sell it. The "moral effect" before referred to, of stocks of raw cotton in warehouse, would not apply in this instance ; for good staple cottons are now so very scarce.

The South does not even get credit for the quantities of cotton which she has contributed to Europe. In addition to what she sent to England last year, she shipped, through the West Indies to the continent of Europe, 15,000 bales—in value equal to 70,000 bales at old prices, and as we know, the Federal manufacturers were also supplied. The British Board of Trade tables only credit the Confederacy with that cotton which is received *direct* from her ports, while all that which is imported *indirectly* is placed to the account of the country of intermediate export. And it is upon these Board of Trade returns that the statesmen and journalists of England have been basing their arguments—laboring under the vain delusion that "other countries" had greatly increased their growth of cotton. The Cotton Supply Association has not had the candor to acknowledge the facts of the case. On the contrary, its "organs" have reproduced, without explanation, the erroneous, or rather misplaced figures furnished by the government; and the Association itself has been publishing weekly the most visionary statements from its correspondents abroad, so ambiguously worded as to deceive the public mind upon the important question of cotton supplies, that many people believe that England has, in a great measure, become independent of the Southern States, as far as the cotton matter is concerned—and this is one reason for the apathy that has existed in England in reference to the Confederate cause for so many months past. If recognition or mediation could only be brought about in time to permit of a good cotton planting in 1865, the finances of the South would be soon righted; but if another season is lost, it will be very inconvenient to the South.

The Manchester Cotton Supply Association, in the whole eight years of its existence, and after spending about £5,000 a year, has never, by its own efforts, succeeded in producing, or getting produced as much as 500 bales of cotton ; and that quantity could have been raised under glass in England, at a less cost than the expenditure of the Association has been. What matters it, if in countries where only a few hundred weights of cotton have been grown, the cultivation should, under the stimulus of high prices, have been augmented

100 or 200 per cent.? The whole additional quantity is but a drop in the bucket, in comparison with the void created by the partial loss of the southern crops. The people of England are very much " at sea" on this cotton question; and it is the duty of the Cotton Supply Association, with its semi-official privileges and reputation, to enlighten them upon the subject. Surely if cotton was being received into England in sufficient supplies for " five days" work in the week, as has been alleged, the prices would tumble back to something resembling their normal condition, instead of being at more than four rates, because the currency in which cotton is quoted is in no manner inflated; and there never was more than "six" working days in the week. The cotton mills, even in the most active times, " rested on the seventh day." The deficiency of only one-sixth of a full supply would not make such an enormous difference in the value as now exists. Cotton has already touched the highest point ever reached. To be sure some New Orleans middling cotton sold at Liverpool during the last war between Great Britain and the United . States (1814), at 39 pence; but that quotation was in paper money, when gold was at a premium of 30 per cent. The specie price, therefore, was but 30 pence per pound.

The truth is, strange as it may seem, the cotton manufacturers of England, although they have done a smaller business in *quantity* since the breaking out of the American war, they have done a greater business in *value*, and their profits were never before so large in any period of three years as since the fall of Fort Sumter. They have had the advantage of gradually hardening prices, while the other classes of the community have assisted them in the support of their idle operatives. Had these operatives been fully employed, the manufacturers themselves would have been ruined, because the world was so largely overstocked with cotton goods. If the American war had been brought to a termination at any time previous to the planting season of 1862, every body in Europe and in the Federal states, interested in cotton, in whatever shape, or wherever held, would have been ruined; for, up to that time, very little of the staple had been destroyed—a fair crop had been reaped in 1861, and cultivation would, of course, upon a return of peace, have been resumed. The sales by the manufacturers of cotton goods for home demand and exportation, taking the custom house returns as a guide from 1858 to 1860, inclusive, were £214,715,927, while those from 1861 to 1863, inclusive, were £240,067,424.

The quantity of raw cotton, cotton yarns and cotton goods, in the whole world—civilized and uncivilized—is believed to have been as follows, at the periods named:

January 1, 1858,	- -	5,000,000,000 pounds.
January 1, 1859,	- -	6,000,000,000 "
January 1, 1860,	- -	7,000,000,000 "
January 1, 1861,	- -	7,500,000,000 "
January 1, 1862,	- -	7,000,000,000 "
January 1, 1863,	- -	5,500,000,000 "
January 1, 1864,	- -	2,500,000,000 "

And on January 1, 1865, the quantity will be further reduced to 1,500,000,000 pounds.

The annual consumption of American cotton, during the decade from 1840 to 1850, averaged 2,400,000 bales each year. The discovery of gold in California and Australia caused a large expansion of commerce. There was a sudden extra demand for the American staple, and the consumption at once rose to 3,000,000 bales per annum, at which it remained until the breaking out of the conflict in America.

In the year 1850, the quantity of American cotton, in the raw state and in manufactured goods at the consuming points, was equivalent to 6,000,000 bales. The crops that followed were:

1851,	-	-	-	- 3,015,029 bales.
1852,	-	-	-	- 3,262,882 "
1853,	-	-	-	2,930,027 "
1854,	-	-	-	2,847,339 "
1855,	-	-	-	- 3,527,845 "
1856,	-	-	-	- 2,939,519 "
1857,	-	-	-	- 3,113,962 "

21,636,603

or, an average of 3,090,943 bales each year; which was just equal to the requirements of mankind. The succeeding crops were:

1858,	-	-	-	- 3,851,481 bales.
1859,	-	-	-	- 4,675,770 "
1860,	-	-	-	- 3,656,086 "

12,183,337

or, an average of 4,061,112 bales per annum. This created an excess of 3,000,000 bales in addition to the stock on hand in 1850, or a total of 9,000,000 bales, nearly the whole of which has now been consumed. The excess, however, was hid from view, in consequence of the raw cotton being converted into goods, there having been an increase in the spinning force of Europe and America, in 1858. 1859 and 1860, of 33¼ per cent. That gave a fictitious demand for raw cotton, and the goods made therefrom met, likewise, a fictitious demand by reason of the impetus given to trade after the close of the Crimean war, the suppression of the mutiny in India, and the settlement of the difficulties in China.

In consequence of so large a proportion of commercial cotton, consisting of the growth of the Southern States, the "bale" became the standard of measure, when speaking of quantity, and that system has been continued up to the present time. But it is just as absurd to estimate the stocks of cotton by that standard now, as it is to value the cost of any article in the Confederacy by the quotation in paper money. American bales average 460 lbs. in weight, but those of India much less. Surats weigh but 370 lbs., and Madras and Bengal only 290 lbs. West India cotton bales contain 200 lbs.; Italy and Malta, 220 lbs.; Brazils, 180 lbs.; Egyptian, 500 lbs.; Turkish, 350 lbs.; Grecian, 200 lbs.; Chinese and Japanese, 120 lbs.; Peruvian, 150 lbs.; African, 150 lbs. The stocks of cotton, as reported, therefore, give a very incorrect view of the quantity; and that incorrect view operates to the prejudice of the Southern States; for it would appear to the uninitiated, when stated in bales, as if the stocks on hand as well as the importations of cotton were greater than they really are.

The actual consumption of cotton has gone steadily on. If there has been any check at all, it has been only in the natural increase that would have taken place these last three or four years, if prices had not advanced. But after peace is restored, there must necessarily be almost as great a bound in the demand as there was when gold was discovered in California and Australia. It may be safe to say that the world can consume on an average 4,500,000 bales of American cotton for each year for the next ten years. The old stocks of the raw material have been so largely drawn upon to make up for the partial stoppage of supplies from the Confederacy, that the warehouses will have to be replenished. Thus, in addition to the actual, there will be, for some years to come, a fictitious consumption for cotton; and prices cannot fall back to their former level until the trade resumes its normal condition in relation to stocks.

It is quite clear that had cultivation been continued uninterruptedly in the South, that prices would not have averaged in the six years from 1861 to 1866, inclusive, over 4 pence per pound. In those six years, 15,000,000,000 pounds would have been used—the low price increasing the consumption—at a cost of £250,000,000 sterling; whereas the chances are that prices within that period may average 16 pence per pound, or more: but if that average price proves correct, the cost to consumers will be, even on a diminution of the quantity to the extent of 25 per cent., by reason of the higher price, £750,000,000. It will then be seen that the American war is thus insidiously inflicting a great loss upon other nations in a pecuniary point of view, to say nothing of the derangement of the system of labor in all those countries, where an increase in the cultivation of cotton has been attempted.

If the war should be brought to a close in time to enable the Southern people to plant cotton seed for 4 or 5,000,000 bales in 1865, the money that will be received for that crop and the crop of 1866, will amount to as large a sum, perhaps larger than would have been the net proceeds of the several crops that have been missed. In this view, it is therefore most important that the war should terminate this winter.

The subjoined is an estimate of the quantity of cotton in the Confederacy, September 1, 1864:

Crop of 1860, remaining over September 1, 1861 :			
At the ports, including 300 bales new crop,	- -	37,574	
In the interior towns,	- - -	6,200	
On the plantations, -	- - -	25,000	
			68,744
Crop of 1861 (estimated), -	- - - -	-	3,500,000
Crop of 1862 " -	- - -	-	1,300,000
Crop of 1863. " -	- - -	-	500,000
Crop of 1864 " -	- - -	-	500,000
			5,868,744
Destroyed and damaged, equal to	(estimated)	- 1,100,000	
Exported and stolen by the Yankees,	"	- 700,000	
Consumed within the Confederacy,	"	- 2,000,000	
			3,800,000
September 1, 1864—bales,			2,068,744

The writer of these pages is frequently asked why the British rulers do not express fears concerning the threatened cotton famine? The answer is, that they have not looked deeply into the subject. The writer greatly regrets that but few persons have taken the pains to investigate the matter. He would have been glad to have had many coadjutors in the attempt to elucidate so important a topic, as it is next to impossible for one person to stem the current of public opinion, no matter how incorrect that opinion may be, when the "leading and governing classes" set it astray. The Queen of England herself, in her last address to Parliament, made an error in stating that "there is every reason to look forward to an increased supply of cotton from various countries which have hitherto but scantily furnished our manufacturers with this material for their industry." Lord Derby, in his speech on the same occasion, made the same mistake. And the British Commissioners of Customs, in their recent report, boast of an extra growth of cotton in the Bahamas, the Bermudas and Mexico, and attempt to verify their assertions by the Board of Trade returns, which, as before remarked, place to the credit of those countries all the Confederate cotton sent thither for reshipment.

It is a remarkable fact, that while England frequently, previous to the difficulties in America, appointed committees from the House of Commons to enquire into the cotton supply, no such committee has been suggested since the war commenced. Possibly something of the kind may be entertained at the coming session. It is well known that an Englishman will not move without an "Act of Parliament."

Up to the present time the Confederacy has had, for the reasons herein named, the people of Manchester against it; and it is natural that the English rulers should withhold the recognition of the South until the persons most immediately interested in the cotton trade should express their opinion in favor of such a policy. The cotton speculators at Liverpool have also thrown cold water upon recognition. So have all those persons engaged in the Indian, Chinese, South American and Egyptian trade: and almost the entire banking interest has been opposed to the South, in consequence of the long established connection with the North. The writer by no means defends the course of the British rulers, but with this explanation, it will be easy to perceive the cause for the tardiness which they have exhibited towards extending to the Confederacy that justice which it has had a right to expect. Recognition is, in truth, not the right word to use. Great Britain, France and all the other powers should have, at the very outset of the secession movement, *received* the accredited ministers from the Southern States under the old treaties, because the Federal Government, unlike the individual states, has never been formally acknowledged as an independent power by any nation on the face of the globe.

It is neither the province nor the wish of the writer to attack Confederate legislation on the subject of cotton; nor yet to intrude his advice upon the Congress of these sovereign States; but he desires to express his opinion that England, unless for some selfish political causes,

4

will never throw the weight of her influence in favor of the South until Manchester speaks, and that Manchester is not likely to speak until the Confederate "cotton leak" is stopped. In ordinary times 4 to 5,000 bales of American cotton reaching Liverpool every week would be inconsiderable; but now that the stocks of raw cotton and cotton goods are so much reduced, that quantity becomes an important feature in the trade of Great Britain. Had the exportation of cotton from the Confederacy been prohibited a year ago, England would by this time have been compelled to acknowledge the independence of the South; for the amount of cotton contributed to Lancashire within the last twelve months has been the means of keeping her mills in partial operation. The position of the cotton trade is quite different now from what it was then, or even two years ago. The British cotton manufacturers will not be content to remain quiet, if they are deprived of the raw material when they have a demand for their fabrics. So long, however, as the Confederacy voluntarily contributes to their wants, it cannot be expected that they will exert themselves to bring about peace.

No particular reference has been made in this paper to that class of cotton known as Sea Island. The quantity of it required is so trifling—only one per cent.—that it is hardly worth while to discuss it. It may be remarked, however, that when the cultivation of Sea Island was extended some years ago, the price fell to such a point that the planters deemed it best for their own interests to place a limit upon its production.

Englishmen vainly congratulate themselves that their country "is no longer mainly dependent upon one source for their cotton supply." They make no allowance for the old stocks of cotton that have been attracted to their shores by the high prices that have ruled. And how, in the name of common sense, can more than one source of supply, as far as quantity is concerned, be kept up? The cotton growers of the world produce cotton for the purpose of selling it—not for keeping it on hand to make England "independent" of the Southern States. So, if the planters in other countries could not find at all times a ready market for their staple, they would soon cease to cultivate it: and Englishmen themselves are not inclined to purchase more cotton than they want, year after year, even if there was cotton to sell in those other countries. In alluding to America as a grower of cotton, it has been the habit of Englishmen to speak in the singular. They talk of the hardship of "one source of supply," when, in truth, that supply, instead of being from "one source," is contributed by *twelve* sovereign states.

It will be remembered that shortly after the Confederate victories in front of Richmond in the summer of 1862, the British government, it was reported, had determined to acknowledge the independence of these States. An intimation was not only thrown out to that effect by the friends of the Ministry, but Mr. Gladstone, the Chancellor of the Exchequer, in his speech at New Castle, conveyed the same idea to the public. His remarks, in fact, savored so much of recognition, that the Lancashire people became alarmed, and exerted their influence in order to prevent the government taking such a step. Those Lancashire people, and with them may be included the Yankee and Confederate cotton speculators, were large holders of raw cotton and cotton goods, and they feared that the opening of the Southern ports would be the means of deluging them with cotton, and lowering the value of what they held. No such fear, however, now exists. The same interests are now well cleared of their stocks, and they know that the quantity of cotton now in the Confederacy is very much less than the amount they estimated to be on the plantations over two years ago. No opposition, therefore, need be again expected from that quarter. On the contrary, the position of the trade is at present so different from what it was then, that they may be expected to urge the government to interpose, so that the mills will be able to resume, as far as possible, their accustomed work. The importance then, of shutting off the Confederate contributions of cotton, will no doubt be apparent to every one. The mill owners, hitherto, have been assisted, in the support of their idle operatives, by persons of every class in the Kingdom. That assistance was cheerfully proffered, under the belief that the mill owners were actual sufferers by the so-called "cotton famine." But now that it is known that the cotton lords have been making money by the short supply of the raw material, forcing up the values of their old stocks, the other classes of the community will be very loth to aid them in continuing their work people in idleness. Nor will the spinners and manufacturers themselves remain quiet: About one hundred millions of pounds sterling are invested directly in mills and machinery, to say nothing of entire villages, whose rental depends upon the earnings of persons employed in the production of cotton goods. The railway and various other interests are likewise deeply concerned in having a renewal of the supplies of the American staple. Great Britain cannot conduct her India trade successfully without the support of Southern cotton. Her exports to that country, in 1863 amounted to £20,000,000, of which £14,000,000, or more than two-thirds, was composed of cotton goods. The kinds of goods most in use in India have to be made out of American cotton—none other will answer, as has been shown in this paper. Should the supply of good staple cotton fall off, India will again take to making all the goods she requires for her own wants. Although she cannot increase her "growing" force, she can, by a greater use of machinery, augment her spinning force. It never has paid, and never will pay to import cotton from India into England, and to export it back from England to India in the manufactured state. The cotton that India parts with is consumed by the inhabitants of other countries.

It may seem strange, but it is nevertheless the fact, that most of the cotton spinners and manufacturers of Lancashire, have been investing their profits of the last few years in the erection of new mills and machinery—thus giving partial employment to their discharged operatives who have not been engaged on the public works; and at the same time placing themselves in a position to enter the cotton markets for additional supplies of the raw material so soon as the war is brought to a termination. The people of Lancashire, it will thus be seen, have no notion of abandoning the cotton trade. If such an idea had entered their heads, they would have invested their earnings of the past four years in something else than bricks and mortar, and spindles and power looms. The fact is, that while England was doing her full share of the cotton *manufacturing* business of the world, she was gradually monopolizing the *spinning* business of mankind. She has already become a gigantic "spinster." In the six years, 1858 to 1863, she exported 935,283,589 pounds of twist and yarn, against a net importation of raw cotton of 4,771,876,480 pounds. After making an allowance for the loss of weight in spinning, it will be ascertained that nearly one-fourth of the net importations of cotton into England were re-exported in twist and yarn. With the large amount of capital invested in cotton spinning and manufacturing establishments, and with the advantage of her moist climate, so well suited for the fabrication of the staple of the South, England is the commercial as well as the natural ally of the Confederate States. Her rulers will soon be compelled to admit that important truth.

With the aid of all the influence of the statesmen of Europe, all the power of the leading capitalists, and all the energy of the mercantile community, other countries have not increased their production since 1860, over 350,000 bales. That small quantity may well be called a "miserable pittance," in comparison with the partial loss of the Southern crops. The Southern States, prior to the war, yielded two-thirds of all the cotton grown in the world, and furnished three-fourths of all that which entered the channels of commerce.

The subjoined table gives the

Tariff Duties on American Cotton—1864.

COUNTRIES.	QUANTITIES.	RATES OF DUTY.
Great Britain,	– ·	Free.
France,	220 lbs.	$ 3 92 (20 francs).
Spain,	101 lbs.	In national vessels, 79½; foreign, $1 85.
Russia,	36 lbs.	1⅜ cents.
Bremen,	Ad valorem.	⅝ of 1 per cent.
Sardinia,	–	Free.
Belgium,	–	Free.
Austria,	–	Free.
Sweden and Norway,	–	In Sweden, free; in Norway, nearly ¼ per cent.
Mexico,	101 lbs.	$1 50.
Hamburg,	Ad valorem.	½ of 1 per cent.
Holland,	–	Free.
Two Sicilies.	192.50 lbs.	$ 8.
Br. N. A. Possessions,	–	Free.
Denmark,	–	Free.
Portugal,	101 lbs.	21.5 cents.
Tuscany,	–	Free.
Papal States,	74.86 lbs.	10 cents.
Cuba,	101 lbs.	In national vessels, 19½; in foreign vessels, 27½ per cent., on a valuation of $5.

	Per Census—Bales of 400 lbs. each.	Per Prices Current—Actual Number of Bales.
Illinois,	6	
Missouri,	100	
Kentucky,	4 092	
Virginia,	12 727	56 987, part grown in North Carolina.
Florida,	63 322	192 794, part grown in Georgia.
North Carolina,	145 514	41 194, some shipped through Va. and S. C.
Tennessee,	227 450	108 676, some included with Louisiana.
South Carolina,	353 413	510 109, part grown in N. C. and Georgia.
Arkansas,	367 485	– included with Louisiana.
Texas,	405 100	252 424, some included with Louisiana.
Georgia,	701 840	525 219, some included with South Carolina.
Louisiana,	722 218	2 139 425, part grown in other States.
Alabama,	997 978	843 012
Mississippi,	1 195 699	– included with Louisiana.
	5 196 944 bales.	4 669 770 bales of 445 lbs.
At 400 lbs. each,	2 078 777 600 lbs.	2 078 047 650 lbs.

The production of cotton in other countries than the Southern States, cannot be increased beyond the yield of 1864. The high prices that have ruled have already stimulated cultivation to the utmost extent possible, and that extra cultivation, as already stated, does not give to the world more than 350,000 bales beyond the quantity grown in 1860, or less than one-tenth of the ordinary supply of the Confederacy. Cotton cultivation is a question of labor as well as soil and climate.

India ranks as the second cotton producing country; yet her entire yield does not exceed 2,000,000 bales of light weight and inferior quality. She exports about one-half of what she grows. An English traveler, who returned from India last year, says:

Cotton in most parts of India is cultivated in rotation with other crops, and is seldom looked upon as the main stay of the ryot, but only as a subordinate product. The great staple of cultivation every where is breadstuffs, in some shape or another. The holdings of the ryots are extremely small, and it has been the custom from time immemorial for each individual to raise sufficient food for his own family. In addition to this, he may grow a little plot of cotton, yielding on the average one or two bales But the ryot will not neglect the raising of food for the sake of cotton, however high its price may be. No surplus stocks of grain are available to meet an emergency of this kind; the internal commerce of India is still in the crudest possible shape; no such thing exists as large districts devoted to special branches of agriculture, and drawing their food from some other. The rule, speaking generally, all over India, is for each locality to raise its own supplies of food, and for each separate cultivator to do the same for himself. So true is this that, if the grain crops fail in any one region, a famine ensues, and people perish by thousands, even though the rest of India is unaffected. During the famine in the Northwestern Provinces in 1861, half a million of people are said to have died from starvation, while in the most of India the crops were not deficient; but so wretched were the means of internal communication, and so little was the trade in breadstuffs organized, that supplies could not be thrown into the famished districts in time to avert this awful calamity It is not, then, to be wondered that the natives are reluctant to diminish their food crops in order to turn their land into cotton.

Mr. W. Wanklyn, the gentleman who had charge of the cotton samples in the International exhibition of 1862, says:

Next the ginning. The American uses for the Sea Island the Macarthy gin, and all evidence goes to prove that this gin is the best, and the only gin which does not injure long staples. These are Sea Island, Brazilian and Egyptian; it also cleans New Orleans with less injury than the saw gin, but does less quantity, and therefore is not in favor.

The saw gin injures all cottons except American and African. It chops East Indian to bits. The best implement for East Indian or other short stapled is, I think, Platt's or Dunlop's, or Dobson and Barlow's gins; but this is a question which at present is not by any means decided. Ginning is a very important affair, for I can show cotton worth 13d. per pound cleaned in a proper machine, and the same cotton, having been put through an improper machine, worth only 8d.

The *London Examiner,* a journal in no manner in the interest of the Confederate cause, utters the following candid words in reference to Indian cotton:

It appears, then, that after ransacking the whole temperate and tropical world, from Italy to Japan, and giving enormous bounties for cotton, our present supply is equal to no more than three and a half days out of six of the quantity necessary to work our looms in employ. Supposing that no increase in our supply had taken place for three years, which would be contrary to the experience of fifty years, our supply was, short last year of what it was in 1861, or before the American civil war, in the proportion of seven to twelve, or a deficit running close upon one-half. The full supply of 1861 cost us about £30,000,000, and the present year (1864), scant one, it is estimated, will cost us not less than £80,000,000; so that for the scant supply we are paying about three times what we did for the full one. India is the country which has furnished us with the largest supply to make up for the loss of the American cotton; but India, as we always predicted in this journal, will never supply the place of America, and its failure to do so has been most exemplary. In 1861, the price of Surat, or the best Indian cotton, in the Liverpool market, was from 3¼. to 4d. a pound; it ranges at present at from 1s. 8d. to 1s. 11d. a pound, so that we are really paying a bounty of some 500 per cent. on the nominal price; and what has been the result? In 1861, India supplied us with 968,000 bales of cotton, and last year with 1,220,000, a paltry increase of no more than 26 per cent.; and this, too, is not the produce of increased growth, but the result of withdrawing the large supply formerly sent to China, and sweeping the India market of all manner of rubbish, raising the cost enormously to the Indian wearer and consumer. As to the quality of Indian cotton, it has not only undergone no improvement, but suffered a great deterioration. "Indian cotton," said Mr. Cheetham, at the Manchester meeting, "was never more contemptible, in the opinion of the manufacturer and workmen, than at the present moment."

The *Edinburgh Review,* a periodical that cannot be charged with having any partiality for the South, thus honestly expresses itself:

Already the intensity of the demand has induced strange devices to meet it, and has inflicted distress upon more than one class of the native community. Not only have the warehouses at Mirzapore and other marts of trade been emptied of their old and probably damaged stock, but all the rubbish that could be got together and screwed into bales, including even, it is said, the wadding of furniture, quilts and cloaks, has been shipped to England: circumstances which will account, in some measure, for the complaints of the inferior quality of recent importations. The native spinners and weavers have thus been deprived of a sufficient quantity of the raw material for their own use, and are reduced in some parts of the country to extreme distress. But for a happy demand for labor upon railways and other public works, their sufferings would have been still more severe. The people of the northern and other more elevated parts of the country, whose dress and coverlets in the cold season are mainly composed of cotton fabrics, quilted with cotton wool, have been put to very great inconvenience, to say the least, by the extremely high price to which an article of such prime necessity has risen.

Egypt stands third on the list as a cotton exporting country. She, however, has, under the influence of high prices, reached her maximum yield—about 300,000 bales—and in doing so, has so diverted her system of labor, that she has been obliged to become an importer of grain from her neighbors. Thus, there was a famine in the land of Egypt this year. not owing, however, to a non-supply of water from the Nile, but in consequence of the scarcity of labor. Mr. Samuel Smith, who visited Egypt a short time since, writes: "Indeed, the only circumstances which limit the spread of cotton culture, are want of water and scarcity of labor." Mr. Smith states that the water can be procured by cutting new canals; but he does not suggest any method by which additional labor can be obtained. Cotton, in

Egypt, is a very exhausting crop, and cannot be grown successively on the same soil; it can only be raised in alternate years with advantage.

Brazil is the next largest grower of cotton. Nearly the whole of her exportations are sent to Great Britain, to which country she contributed in 1863, 56,508 bales of 400 pounds each, against 58,347 bales in 1862; 43,226 bales in 1861; 43,217 bales in 1860; 56,197 bales in 1859, and 46,545 bales in 1858. It is probable that the returns for 1864 will show a slight increase in the quantity of cotton received from Brazil, as she is now pretty well drained of her old stocks. There has been no increase of moment in production there, or in any other sugar growing country, owing to the scarcity of labor. To be sure, a country like Brazil could increase her production of cotton, by importing Coolie labor; but then it would take many years to obtain a sufficient number of Chinese to make any important addition to the agricultural force of Brazil.

I have already alluded to the fact, that China is not naturally a cotton exporting country, though she sent to England in 1863 and 1864 considerable quantities, for the reasons stated, namely—a reduction of her stock of raw cotton, in consequence of the high prices that have prevailed, and also owing to her markets having been overcrowded with cotton goods, manufactured chiefly from American cotton. China, unlike the other cotton growing countries, has an abundance of labor, but an insufficient area of soil for cultivation. Her condition in this respect will be explained by the following extract from Sir John Bowring's letter, dated Government House, Hong Kong, 13th July 1855, and addressed to the Registrar General at London:

I think there is abundant evidence of redundant population pressing more and more heavily upon, and suffering more and more severely from an inadequate supply of food. Though there are periods when extraordinary harvests enable the Chinese to transport rice, the principal food of the people, from one province to another, and even sometimes to foreign countries, yet of late the importations from foreign countries have been enormous, and China has drawn largely on the Straits, the Phillippines, Siam, and other places, to fill up a vast deficiency in supply. Famine has, notwithstanding, committed dreadful ravages, and the provisions of the imperial granaries have been wholly inadequate to provide for the public wants. It is true, that cultivation has been greatly interfered with by intestinal disorders, and that there has been much destruction by inundations, incendiarism, and other accidental or transitory causes; but without reference to these, I am disposed to believe that there is a greater increase in the numbers of the population than in the home production of the food for their use. It must be remembered, too, that while the race is thus augmenting, the causes which lead to the destruction of food—such as the overflow of rivers, fires, ravages of locusts, bad seasons, and other calamities—are to a great extent beyond the control of human prudence or human exertion. It would be difficult to show what new element could be introduced, which would raise up the native supply of food beyond its present productiveness, considering that hand husbandry has given to cultivation more of a horticultural than an agricultural character. * * * * In all parts of China to which we have access, we find not only that every foot of ground is cultivated which is capable of producing any thing, but that, from the value of the land and the surplus of abor, cultivation is rather that of gardeners than of husbandmen. The sides of hills, in their natural declivity, often unavailable, are, by a succession of artificial terraces, turned to profitable account. Every little bit of soil, though it be only a few feet in length and breadth is turned to account; and not only is the surface of the land thus cared for, but every device is employed for the gathering together of every article that can serve for manure. * * * * The multitudes of persons who live by the fisheries in China, afford evidence not only that the land is cultivated to the greatest possible extent, but that it is insufficient to supply the necessities of the overflowing population; for agriculture is held in high honor in China, and the husbandman stands next in rank to the sage or the literary man in the social hierarchy. It has been supposed that nearly a tenth of the population derive their means of support from fisheries.

This statement of Sir John Bowring makes the fact quite clear that China cannot increase her growth of cotton, and that now that she has permitted herself to be drained of the raw material, she must necessarily resume her position as an importer of cotton from India. If cotton could be grown upon the water, China might increase her yield, but the laws of nature will not be set aside to oblige the Lancashire mill owners.

The importations of cotton from China into England, were in 1862 4,415 bales, and in 1863, equal to 77,140 bales of 400 pounds each. In 1864, the quantity was somewhat larger; but in 1865 it is not probable there will be any receipts from that source.

Japan, like China, is an overpopulated country, and holds the same position in respect to cotton. Yet she, for similar reasons, was enabled to send to England, in 1863, 1,779 bales of 400 pounds each, and in 1864, an increase on that quantity. It is hardly possible that she can spare any cotton in 1865.

Turkey, both in Europe and in Asia, has made great efforts to augment her yield of cotton. She sent to England, in 1858, 28 bales of 400 pounds each; in 1859, 994 bales; in 1860, 31 bales; 1861, 177 bales; 1862, 11,539 bales; 1863, 30,882 bales. In 1864, the quantity recorded by the British returns to the credit of Turkey will be much less than in 1863, owing partly to the fact that France received a portion of the supplies from that country, and partly to the fact that the shipments of 1863 consisted in a great measure of old stocks of cotton. One of the British Consuls in Turkey thus writes, under date of December 31, 1862:

The cotton grown here is of a very inferior quality, and has never been found good enough for the manufacture of twist, the staple being too short. The amount exported to France and Italy was chiefly used for making wicks and stuffing furniture. In the present scarcity in Europe, however, manufacturers were driven to make use of it, mixed with other better qualities. This caused a sudden demand for it in France, and all that existed in the market was bought up immediately, at double prices. The demand still continuing after the stock of the year's produce had been bought up, the old cotton, that had for many years served for stuffing mattresses, pillows and divans, was brought to the market, and disposed of at high prices.

The cultivation of cotton in the West India Islands and adjacent countries does not increase. A report made by the committee of the Cotton Supply Association gives the following excuses for the small production: "Barbadoes cannot produce any large quantity of cotton without throwing sugar out of cultivation." "The commissioner from British Guiana does not hold out much hope of an extensive revival of the cultivation of cotton in that territory, unless English capitalists will undertake to find the means of developing the latent resources of the country. At present, however, sugar offers greater inducements. Chinese laborers might be introduced with great advantage." "Costa Rica sends samples of wild cotton, of good useful quality, but they cannot be considered more than botanical specimens." "Ecuador sends four or five samples of very good, clean cotton, but at present the quantity cultivated is too small to be of much benefit." In Martinique, " it is said that the culture there will never be considerable." Guadaloupe is pretty much in the same condition. " Cotton has been cultivated in French Guiana for many years, but the want of labor, and the more remunerative prices for other products, have depressed its cultivation." In Hayti, "the land available is sufficient to grow 3,000,000 bales a year, but there would be a deficiency of labor." Jamaica presents the same excuse for her shortcomings as to the supply of cotton. Trinidad is not "likely" to send "any great quantity," "unless English energy and capital are employed." Uraguay furnishes a few "purely experimental samples, but they are evidence that good cotton grows in the vicinity of the great rivers of South America; and the merchants of Montevideo and Buenos Ayres ought to encourage and develop the production of this cotton." Venezuela grows a few hundred bales of cotton; and the best that can be said for her, is that "it is *probable* that the increase in cultivation will be larger;" but the "probability" has not been realized. St. Christopher exported in 1863 but 5 or 6 bales of 400 pounds each; Antigua, only 18 bales; St. Lucia, 3 bales; St. Vincent, 178 bales; Tobago, 8 bales. There is very little cotton grown in Cuba and the other Spanish islands; what is produced in them is nearly all sent to the mother country.

Peru in 1863 exported to England about 46 bales of 400 pounds each, and a similar quantity to France. Peru has distinguished herself more for the age, than for the quantity of her cotton. She contributed to the International Exhibition of 1862, a fleece of cotton weighing about 40 pounds, which had been found in a tomb in one of the ancient ruins of a city which existed before the Spaniards invaded the country. The cotton was of good staple and strong, although over 300 years old.

The whole of Africa, excepting the Cape of Good Hope, contributed only 321 bales of 400 pounds each in 1863. The Cape of Good Hope is credited with 9,476 bales of 400 pounds each in the same year, but it is likely that a large share of that quantity was of East India growth, reshipped from thence.

Australia makes a very poor show—Victoria, New South Wales and Queensland combined furnished to the mother country in 1863 but 71 bales of 400 pounds each The commissioner from Queensland to the International Exhibition feared that cotton grown in that country would "not pay for the cost of land and labor." A Queensland correspondent of the London Times writes:

Under certain regulations, we are, it is true, permitted to import labor from India, but Coolie wages are now so dear, and Coolie physique so deficient, that at best that class of labor is expensive. Having personally employed both Coolies and Africans, I should, for most employments, prefer the latter, at double the wages of the former Why again, then, is it that our government forbids the importation of the African to our Colonies?

Queensland gave but 45 bales of cotton of 300 pounds each, notwithstanding the governor of the colony, as far back as the early part of 1861, endeavored to encourage its growth by a bonus of £10 on each bale of that weight of Sea Island, and £5 on every bale of other description of cotton grown there. The bounty, however, was to be in operation but three years.

Spain forwarded about 300 bales of 400 pounds each of cotton to England in 1863. Malta, 952 bales, and Greece, 864 bales. These

5

countries have always produced a little cotton for their own use. So has Italy. She exported to England in 1863, 1,500 bales of 400 pounds each, and a larger quantity to France. Her whole yield, augmented under the influence of high quotations, is estimated at 40,000 bales. Notwithstanding the fostering care of the French government, and the large premiums offered for the cultivation of cotton, the quantity produced in Algeria is said to not exceed 5,000 bales.

There has been very little increase in the production of wool, flax, silks and other textile materials. An erroneous belief exists in the public mind in reference to this subject. It is generally thought that the importations of those materials into England have been enormous, and that they, since the establishment of the blockade, have made up for the deficiency in the cotton supply. This is not the case. They have only assisted to a very slight degree. The increase in the receipts is trifling, in comparison with the falling off in the imports of cotton. Here are the particulars of import:

Flax, Dressed and Undressed.

1858,	-	-	-	143,797,360 pounds.
1859,	-	-	-	160,388,144 "
1860,	-	-	-	164,058,720 "
1861,	-	-	⁄ -	149,372,048 "
1862,	-	-	-	201,415,202 "
1863,	-	-	-	163,037,744 "

Wool.

1858,	-	-	-	126,738,723 pounds.
1859,	-	-	-	133,284,634 "
1860,	-	-	-	148,396,577 "
1861,	-	-	-	147,172,841 "
1862,	-	-	-	171,943,472 "
1863,	-	-	-	177,377,664 "

Hemp, Dressed and Undressed.

1858,	-	-	-	99,302,672 pounds.
1859,	-	-	-	118,621,328 "
1860,	-	-	-	86,019,696 "
1861,	-	-	-	86,187,760 "
1862,	-	-	-	102,570,384 "
1863,	-	-	-	119,606,256 "

Silk.

1858,	-	-	-	6,635,845 pounds.
1859,	-	-	-	10,318,353 "
1860,	-	-	-	9,402,982 "
1861,	-	-	-	8,835,255 "
1862,	-	-	-	10,434,350 "
1863,	-	-	-	9,280,528 "

Jute.

1858,	-	-	-	82,665,520 pounds.
1859,	-	-	-	118,864,160 "
1860,	-	-	-	91,480,146 "
1861,	-	-	-	101,258,304 "
1862,	-	-	-	107,942,688 "
1863,	-	-	-	136,979,696 "

Estimate of Stock of Raw Cotton and Cotton Goods at the consuming points, reduced to Bales of 400 pounds each.

September 1, 1861, on hand, equal to bales, - - -		13,500,000
Usual receipts from other countries for three years (1862, 1863 and 1864), -		4,500,000
Extra growth of other countries:		
1862, - - - - -	50,000	
1863, - - - - -	200,000	
1864, - - - - -	350,000	
		600,000
Southern States contributed in three years (to summer of 1864), -		700,000
		19,300,000
Actual consumption from September 1, 1861, to September 1, 1864, -		14,300,000
Less by 8,500,000 bales than in 1861, or - - -		5,000,000

Estimate for 1865.

Contributions from other countries, - - -	1,200,000	
Contributions from Confederacy, - - -	300,000	
		1,500,000
		6,500,000
Consumption September 1, 1864, to September 1, 1865, - -		5,000,000
At consuming points September 1, 1865, bales, - - -		1,500,000

It will be seen by this statement that the stock of raw cotton and cotton goods at the consuming points, was, on September 1st, 1861, equal to 13,500,000 bales of 400 lbs. each; that on September 1, 1864, the stock had been reduced to equivalent to 5,000,000 bales; and that the stock, on September 1, 1865, will be further reduced to 1,500,000 bales. A very small quantity indeed of cotton and cotton goods!

It is quite manifest that the cotton famine will be reached some time during the coming year. It has only been staved off by the steady arrivals of 4 to 5,000 bales per week of American cotton in England, and that which has been received in the Federal States. While legislation on the subject would have been of little avail early in the conflict, when the stocks of cotton and cotton goods were so large at the consuming points, a prohibition of its exportation from the Confederacy now cannot help but act as a great political lever to draw justice from the "neutral" powers of Europe. 200,000 to 300,000 bales of American cotton, more or less, would hardly, in ordinary times, make an appreciable difference in value, but at the present period that quantity becomes of great moment to the manufacturing interests of the world, as it enables the use of the inferior sorts to five or six times the amount. This paper, it is hoped, will fully explain the reason why the cotton famine has been postponed, and demonstrate that the increase in production in other countries has been trifling indeed, notwithstanding the great stimulus of high prices. While, therefore, it is admitted that "other countries" have, under hot-bed influences, grown 350,000 bales more cotton than in 1860, that quantity seems insignificant in comparison with the yearly advance in the cultivation that has taken place in the Southern States of America, even when unaided by any additional

value to the product. The increase in the cultivation in these States
was as follows :

In 1859 over 1858,	-	-	-	823,929 bales, averaging 450 lbs.
In 1859 over 1857,	-	-	-	1,561.808 " " "
In 1859 over 1856,	-	-	-	1,736,251 " " "

People generally on both sides of the Atlantic have been deceived
as to the production of cotton in other countries, owing to the extra
importations the last three years. The chief portion of these importations consisted of old stocks of cotton, much of which had
actually been used for household purposes. While the inhabitants of
the Eastern countries were emptying their beds, mattresses, divans,
saddles, etc. of raw cotton, the citizens of the Confederacy were
parting with their blankets, and other woolen fabrics, in order to supply the army. It is likely, too, that in the Northern States much of
the cotton that had entered into consumption has again been placed
upon the wheels of commerce. It will be remembered that one of
the passengers on board the ill-fated steamer Lexington, burned on
Long Island Sound in 1840, saved himself by floating on a bale of
cotton, which he afterwards converted into an "ottoman." The
value of the cotton became so great recently, that the owner has
been tempted to part with it. This incident exemplifies the present
position of the commerce in cotton.

Viewing, then, all the circumstances connected with the cotton
trade, it is quite evident that the demand for that material upon the
recurrence of peace, will be greater than previous to the war. All
the channels that have been drained of the staple will have to be
filled up, and an unprecedented call will be made upon these States
to furnish cotton material to the rest of the world. This war has
greatly deranged the course of commerce and finance. That derangement, however, has hardly been felt by those not immediately engaged in the conflict. But the time is coming when, for the happiness
and comfort of future generations, the statesmen of the day will
find it necessary to engraft upon their principles and conduct the
very highest and most stringent rules of political economy. Any attempt to disregard these maxims, the force of which in calmer times
has been acknowledged, will end in ruin and destruction, and discomfort not only to our neighbors, remote as well as immediate, but to
ourselves.

Previous to the American war, the British House of Commons
frequently expressed great concern about the cotton supply, fearing
that, at some future period, there would be an insurrection among
the slaves in the South, and that cotton cultivation would therefore
be suspended. Every few years there was a committee appointed
by that body to investigate the subject. Strange to say, however,
that since the year 1858 the matter has been dropped, and many, if
not the majority of Englishmen, are now laboring under the delusion
that their country has become independent of these States for a supply of that material. The very last official publication—the report
of the " Commissioners of Her Majesty's Customs," before alluded
to—says :

The increase, however, in the quantities of cotton imported from other countries than the United States, is nearly 1,400,000 cwts., viz: from 4,551,581 cwts. to 5,921,332 cwts. From this must be deducted the quantity received from the Bahamas and from our North American Provinces, which has been almost entirely the produce of the Southern States, conveyed to us indirectly through those countries. But even after this deduction is made, the result is very satisfactory, as showing the great and successful efforts that have been made to render this country independent, for the future, of the supply on which she formerly entirely relied.

The Commissioners seem to overlook the fact, that the cotton which was received from the Bermudas, Mexico, Cuba, &c., was all of southern growth ; and they make no allowance either for the old stocks of all the eastern countries, or for the contents of beds, pillow cases, saddles, divans, &c. that have been placed in bales, and resumed the character of merchandise. The prediction of the Commissioners that England would become "independent" of the Southern States for her cotton supply, might, in a measure, prove to be correct, if the "fragments" of all the old stocks of raw cotton, and that which had been used for household purposes, were "gathered up, so that nothing might be lost," and that those "fragments" could be made to perform the miracle of the "loaves and fishes." But as cotton will not grow without being planted and cultivated, it is quite certain that England must again bow down to the commercial monarch.

The writer of this paper believes that there is more than sufficient negro labor in these States to supply the wants of the world with cotton. Should his views in this respect be incorrect, he can see no objection to importing as many Africans as may be required for the purpose, taking them from barbarism and placing them in good and comfortable homes. Under any circumstances, he would not, were he a legislator, consent to make treaties with other powers for the suppression of the African slave trade, unless those other powers would agree at the same time to abandon the Coolie trade, which is, practically, the same kind of commerce.

The "horrors" of the African slave trade were never inaugurated until that trade ceased to be profitable. It was then that the vessels were over-crowded with passengers ; and the same system has been continued, in an aggravated degree, since the trade was made illegal. There is no reason why colored passengers should not be transported across the seas just as decently as Irish, German or Chinese passengers. The writer does not mean by these remarks to advocate the reopening of the African slave trade. He, as just stated, believes there is still left in the South an abundance of negro labor. If such be the case, it would be quite as absurd to import into the Confederacy Africans from Africa as it would be to introduce into Ireland, among her over-crowded peasantry, Germans from Germany.

The British people understand this question of labor thoroughly— they have bought their experience. They see the blunder they made in emancipating the negroes in the West India Islands. In the House of Lords, on May 28, 1861, it was stated by the Duke of Newcastle in answer to Lord Brougham, that the government did not intend to stimulate the production of cotton in the colonies by bounties or any direct remuneration, but that more energetic measures would be taken to promote the emigration of Coolies, in order to supply the want of labor in the West Indies and other colonial countries.

The remarks in this paper, so far, have been confined chiefly to the course of the commerce in cotton with the producing countries, and to the state of the British cotton trade and cotton manufactures. Incidental allusion has likewise been made to the positions of the cotton interest in some of the other manufacturing countries. A further explanation of this last named branch of the cotton question may not be out of place at this juncture—the eve, to all appearances, of a cotton crisis.

France quite as early as England commenced the manufacture of cotton into textile fabrics. Both countries, until the improvements in spinning machinery were invented, mixed the staple with wool or flax. France, however, failed to keep pace with England, though her government from the time of Colbert, the first minister under Louis XIV, tried, by a system of protection, to foster that species of industry. With a few trifling exceptions, of which the cotton lace of Belgium is the only one worthy of notice, foreign cotton *goods* were not admitted into France between the peace of 1815 and the Cobden treaty of 1860. Not content with the prohibition so greatly in their favor, her manufacturers have received a bounty of 25 francs per 100 kilogrammes of cotton yarns and cotton goods exported. The duty most extensively operative—that on American cotton—is 20 francs per 100 kilogrammes; the bounty, therefore, is somewhat greater than the duty, even after allowing for the loss in weight by spinning. The cotton from British India, or Indian cotton from British *entrepots*, is now, by the above named treaty, free of duty.

Under the pampering system of protection and monopoly, which for a time gave large profits, the number of cotton mills in France increased during the years 1825, 1826 and 1827, with such rapidity as to augment the supply of goods greatly in excess of the demand. A heavy decline in the value of the fabrics was the result. Many of the mill owners were ruined; many factories were consequently closed, and the credit of those spinners and manufacturers, who managed to weather the financial storm, was much impaired. The operatives, as remarked some pages back, were thrown out of employment, just as has been the case with those of Lancashire the past four years. By the end of 1829 the equilibrium between supply and consumption became nearly restored, when the mills began to resume their former activity. This gleam of prosperity was, however, soon clouded by political disorders, that culminated in the Revolution of July 1830. Then followed the cholera, which committed great ravages among the working population—retarding the prosperity of the country. And it was not until the spring of 1833 that the manufacturing business of France resumed a steady basis. In the meanwhile the British House of Commons had appointed a committee to enquire into the silk trade. In the report of that committee, dated June 22, 1832, will be found the following testimony of Dr. Bowring, who had been sent to France to examine into the subject just as the French have from time to time dispatched persons to England to enquire into the cotton trade. The Doctor was likewise called upon to give information in reference to the cotton manufactures of France. He said:

While, according to the best calculation, 7,000,000 of spindles are employed in England to manufacture more than 240,000,000 pounds of cotton, in France, according to the return of the Commission which reported on the cotton trade, 3,200,000 spindles are employed to manufacture 66,000,000 pounds; so that where the protected French manufacturer produces only 66,000,000 pounds, the unprotected English manufacturer would, with the same number of spindles, produce nearly 110,000,000 pounds; or if the English manufacturer produced at the same rate as the French, instead of 240,000,000 pounds, he would produce only 144,000,000 pounds. In England it is estimated, according to the Parliamentary returns, that 700,000 persons are engaged in the different branches of the cotton manufacture, and they produce nearly four times the quantity which is rendered in France by 550,000 persons, according to the returns of the French Commission: that protection has thus led to the waste of more than two-thirds of the whole amount of labor employed on the protected articles. The French cotton manufacturers have had the benefit of this prohibiting system ever since the peace, and, according to the statement made by their Commission, it cost the country 47,000,000 francs per annum beyond the sum at which the same articles might be imported from England. This is the result of eighteen years' protection, yet the testimony of the French manufacturers is that the very existence of their business is rendered doubtful from year to year. P. 586.

I think that in almost all the articles of taste and fashion, the French possess a superiority of between 30 and 40 per cent. I think the English have a greater superiority than this in trade manufactures, such as cotton, where mechanical aptitude is brought to bear. P. 593.

I have had evidence enough to satisfy me, in the peculiar position in which I was placed, that at the present moment the importation of cotton twist (by smuggling) is from 15,000,000 francs to 20,000,000 francs. I can also speak, from my own personal knowledge, of the large clandestine importations of cotton twist from Switzerland into France. P. 593.

At this moment, of the capital invested in the production of cotton twist, I may state that the great proportion is absolutely lost, and the loss of the rest is inevitable. I have had occasion to examine the operation of the protective system upon a very wide scale, and I state, as a general result, on the details of which I should be able to give evidence to satisfy honorable members, that the protective system has wholly failed in accomplishing any one object for which it was intended. Wherever there are unfavorable circumstances, such as now connected with the cotton twist trade in France, they cannot successfully be subdued by protection. I am satisfied that no industry can or will succeed that is not of natural growth; that all attempts to force industry have been fatal and ruinous to the nations that have made the attempt.

If I had expected that the general state of manufactures in France would have been gone into, I would have brought some information which would show that the situation of the cotton manufacture is discouraging in the extreme; the expressions of distress which have emanated thence are stronger than have ever been heard even in this country. I have now found among my papers an address to the King, presented in the present year from Mulhausen, the seat of one of the largest manufactures in France, the first sentence of which is, "our looms are wholly abandoned, and our laborers without food." The whole number of looms in the district du Nord was stated by Chaptal at 10,000: now, as evidence of the prosperity of that district, I will mention that in March last the cotton manufactory of Rouval-les-Doullens, established only four years ago by a well known individual (who came to England and visited our most approved establishments), at a cost of 1,400,000 francs, was sold for 308,000 francs; there was a sacrifice, therefore, of between 70 and 80 per cent. of the whole invested capital.

Thus the absurdity of protection to domestic manufactures is fully exposed. Yet France persisted in the same practice; and it is only since the adoption of the wise commercial measures of 1860, under the treaty twice before referred to, that she has shown any intention of altering her system.

On the other hand, with the exception of the parliamentary restrictions of 1700, against the importation of Indian silks and printed calicoes, either for apparel or furniture—which were enacted at the instance of her woolen interest—England has never given any protection whatever to her cotton manufactures. In fact, an opposite policy has been pursued. No sooner were there goods made exclusively of cotton in England than the British Government subjected them to unwise taxation. The first fabrics that were made wholly of cotton, were manufactured in 1773. The officers of excise refused to let them pass at the usual duty on home-made goods, of 3 pence per pound, insisting upon an additional duty of 3 pence per pound, on the ground that they were "Indian" calicoes, though manufactured in England; and even the printing of such goods was, by an old law, prohibited. Parliament then, in 1774, passed the following act:

Whereas a new manufacture of stuffs, wholly made of raw cotton wool (chiefly imported from the British plantations), hath been lately set up within this Kingdom, in which manufacture many hundreds of poor people are employed: and whereas the use and wear of printed &c. stuffs wholly made of cotton and manufactured in Great Britain, *ought to be allowed under proper regulations :* and whereas doubts have arisen whether the said new manufactured stuffs ought to be considered as calicoes, and as such, if printed &c. liable to the inland or excise duties laid on calicoes when printed by the existing statutes, whether the use or wearing of the said new manufactured stuffs, when the same are printed &c. are not prohibited by an act passed 7 Geo. II, intituled, an act to preserve and encourage the woolen and silk manufactures of this Kingdom, and for more effectually employing the poor, by prohibiting the use, and wear, of all printed &c. calicoes in apparel, household stuffs, furniture, or otherwise, after the 25th of December 1722. For obviating all such doubts for the future, be it enacted that no greater or higher duty than three pence for every yard in length, reckoning yard wide, shall be imposed on the said manufactured stuffs wholly made of cotton spun in Great Britain when printed.

And be it further enacted, that it shall be lawful for any person to wear any new manufactured stuffs wholly made of cotton when printed.

Mr. Pitt in 1784 imposed additional taxes on the manufacture of printed calicoes. The troubles of a cotton mill owner, in those days, were not confined to the visits of the excisemen. The operatives though fully employed, feared that machinery would eventually, by continued improvements, perform all the labor; and much ruffianly violence was practiced by them. The upper classes fomented these anti-factory outrages, from an apprehension that the multiplication of machinery would throw a number of idle hands upon the parish funds. Subsequently, the manufacturers were persecuted with a series of imposts, in twelve successive rates, all tending to throw the balance in favor of their foreign rivals in that industry. In 1798, an import duty was levied on raw cotton from the Brazils, of 12s. 6d. per 100 lbs.; from the West Indies, of 8s. 9d.; from the Southern States, of 6s. 6d.; and from the East Indies, of 4 per cent. ad valorem. In 1803, an uniform duty of 16s. 8d. per 100 lbs. was fixed for all cotton except Brazilian, which was chargeable with 25s. per 100 lbs. The duties were afterwards occasionally altered until 1815, when 8s. 6d. per 100 lbs. was imposed upon the growth of all countries. Some further changes were made, favorable to East India cotton, from that date until 1833, when the rate was established at 4d. per 112 lbs. on the production of the British possessions, and 2s. 11d. on the yield of foreign countries. The inland taxes on the manufactures of cotton goods were continued. with a partial intermission, until 1831, when they were taken off. Excepting the general increase of 5 per cent. on nearly all custom duties in May 1840, the tariff of 1833 remained unchanged until March 1845, when cotton was admitted into the United Kingdom from all countries, free from any duty. From 1825 to 1845 the differential duty in favor of East India cotton was very considerable.

While it is clear that import duties *on raw produce*, as a general rule, must necessarily come out of the pockets of the producers, the import tax thus placed by the Government of Great Britain upon the importation of cotton worked to the great injury of her spinners and manufacturers, inasmuch as she re-exported, in yarns and goods, three-fourths the cotton she imported in the raw state. The manufacturers of other countries—France among the number—whose governments either admitted cotton free of duty, or relieved them of that charge, by the payment of a bounty on all the cotton fabrics exported, possessed an advantage over those of England. An import tax on raw materials contained in such manufactures as are consumed within a country, is, in reality, harmless, because that tax is indirectly paid by the planter. It is an item against him in the account sales of his produce. But in all cases where goods are made to be exported to foreign markets, the duty operates to the detriment of the manufacturer, in consequence of its being equivalent to a bounty, to the full amount, whatever it may be, to the manufacturers of other countries. It is strange that the statesmen of England were so long opening their eyes to this glaring fact. The heaviest duties on raw cotton existed during the infancy of the British cotton manufactures, and the highest rates were generally on American, the kind chiefly consumed by the mills, and re-exported in the manufactured state to foreign markets. Export duties on all raw materials also indirectly come out of the pockets of the planter, and likewise act as a bounty to the manufacturer, at the place of production. [The writer has discussed this subject of export duties at considerable length in another paper. It is a topic that seems to have been in a great measure neglected by Adam Smith and all his imitators and followers.]

No enlightened government, except England, has ever laid a tax upon the importation of raw cotton, that has not been countervailed by a drawback equal in amount, upon its exportation in the manufactured condition. She always, however, permitted raw cotton to be reshipped without paying duty.

Against these heavy odds, England has prospered in her cotton manufactures, and completely outdistanced France. England, to be sure, has had the advantage of cheaper coal and iron, but she has not had the exclusive benefit. as is supposed, of her improvements in machinery. No sooner was an invention perfected, than it found its way to France, oftentimes through the meshes of the most stringent interdiction, and severest penalties. Nor has England been enabled to purchase her raw materials on better terms than France. Both countries have, since the trade assumed magnitude, depended on the Southern States as the chief source of supply. France had a monopoly of the Louisiana cotton trade, when that country was under her own and the dominion of Spain. At that period, however, but little cotton was cultivated there. The clause in the treaty of

6

purchase, 1803, excluded all foreign powers, except France and Spain, from *importing* goods into the Louisiana territory, "without in any way affecting the regulations that the United States may make concerning the exportations of the produce and merchandise of the United States, or any right they may have to make such regulations." That provision which was limited to twelve years, was probably inserted in order to avoid prejudicing the interests of the established commercial connecti·ns between Spain and France and New Orleans. France had some advantage over England before the age of steam, by her nearer proximity to the cotton growing countries of the Mediterranean, who were the earliest contributors of that article to Western Europe. Then came the West Indies; then, after independence, the Southern States of America; then the East Indies. India, up to 1787, had not exported a ·y raw cotton; in that year 100,000 lbs. were received from her into England, through Ostend. Her shipments of cotton anterior thereto were in the manufactured state. Southern cotton having been cultivated on a larger scale simultaneously with the improvements in spinning machinery, revolutionized the cotton trade of the world. Cotton has been occasionally grown in the south of France, in small quantities, since its introduction there from Italy about 300 years ago. Napoleon in 1807, appreciating its importance, endeavored to promote its culture.

France is the only country in Europe that can, in any sense, pretend or claim to compete with England in respect to the spinning of yarn and the manufacture of cotton goods. But when the character and development of that industry in the respective countries is compared, it will be readily seen that France, unlike England, offers no extended market for the produce of the Southern States. France consumes annually within her own borders about 150,000,000 pounds of cotton for clothing her people, while nearly double that quantity is so used by the people of the British isles. The exports of cotton manufactures of all kinds from France reach only one-tenth the value of those sent from England to other parts. As India is the largest market for the productions of British cotton looms, so is Algeria the principal importer of those of France. They each take about one-fourth the entire exportations of cotton goods from either country. The French cotton goods sold in the English and American markets, owe their value rather more to the designer and the dyer than to the planter or weaver. Their consumption, therefore, does not admit of any very rapid or wide increase. French taste and French chemistry, wherever they are applicable, have deservedly won for French textile fabrics a superiority universally recognized.

The extent of the cotton manufactures of France will be seen by reference to tables F and G. A few particulars may, however, be here introduced. The average quantity of raw cotton imported into France, and retained for the use of her mills in the five years, 1848 to 1852, was about 132,000,000 pounds. She likewise bought cotton yarns, chiefly from England, to a value of about 700,000 francs per annum. In 1853, her net receipts of raw cotton were increased to 165,000,000 pounds, valued at 125,000,000 francs, and her imports of yarns were worth 1,400,000 francs. The cotton goods exported from France in 1853 were cleared at a valuation of 71,900,000 francs, and her cotton yarn at 866,000 francs. These amounts exhibit but a slight increase on the average of the five previous years. The cotton trade of France for 1859, 1860, 1861, 1862 and 1863, figured as follows:

A Statement of the French Commerce in Raw Cotton, 1859 to 1863.

YEARS.		Importations.	Exportations.	Excess of Imports.	Net Value.	American Portion.
		Lbs.	Lbs.	Lbs.	Francs.	Lbs.
1859,	-	201 901 408	22 238 146	179 663 264	153 741 989	179 600 000
1860,	-	306 675 848	34 535 257	272 140 591	202 710 114	252 667 555
1861,	-	282 432 832	11 022 145	271 410 687	270 631 594	241 445 321
1862,	-	101 842 286	16 413 960	85 428 325	126 157 880	437 573
1863,	-	141 580 298	19 480 813	122 099 485	177 168 499	10 000
		1 034 432 672	103 690 321	930 742 352	930 410 076	674 210 449

It will be seen by the third column of the preceding table, that the excessive importations of raw cotton into France in 1859, 1860 and 1861, enabled her to manage without a full supply in 1862 and 1863. The net importations for the whole period made a fair average—186,148,470 pounds per annum. France, like England, also held a large reserve of cotton goods in 1861. That reserve is now reduced to a low point. So long as the old supply lasted, France, as a community, hardly felt the pressure of high prices. On the contrary, the light outlay for cotton in 1862, made her easy in money matters, and enabled her to stand the drain upon her resources, created by the large importations of grain that year, in order to meet the deficiency arising from the bad harvest of 1861. In place of buying cotton, she purchased wheat. France on no former occasion drew breadstuffs from abroad in such quantities, without feeling great financial embarrassment. The usual expense to the people of France for the raw cotton contained in their clothing, is one hundred and twenty millions of francs per annum. In 1865, that material will cost them upwards of five hundred millions of francs, unless prices should be much reduced by the opening of the Southern ports. Of the quantity of raw cotton received into France, there was imported through English ports (per British Board of Trade returns), in

1858,	5,261,200	pounds, valued at	£148.183
1859,	7,437,888	" "	185,693
1860,	13,028,848	" "	306,610
1861,	12,487,440	" "	371,926
1862,	61,238,576	" "	3,737,366
1863,	80,000,000	" "	5,317,543

France sent to England in the same years (per British Board of Trade returns), viz :

1858,	5,264,560 pounds, valued at		£157,160
1859,	3,349,136 " "		100,255
1860,	2,186,688 " "		62,562
1861,	955,172 " "		38,840
1862,	5,491,248 " "		327,323
1863,	1,683,696 " "		160,108

The raw cotton exported from England to France in 1861, 1862 and 1863, was of the growth of the undermentioned countries :

	1861.	1862.	1863.
Growth of Southern States, - -	216 503	703 577	329 259
Brazil, - - -	2 951	87 085	50 820
Egypt, - - -	16 590	118 381	149 426
British India, - -	135 882	2 810 636	4 582 548
Other countries, - -	–	17 687	205 490
Total, -	£ 371 926	£ 3 737 366	£ 5 317 543

It will be noticed by these tables that France carries on both an importing and an exporting trade in raw cotton with England. She, however, buys more cotton from, than she sells to England. Her exports thither of that article consist principally of the American staple, of which sort she sometimes imports more than she needs. Her supplies from England of late are mostly of Indian cotton. Under the Cobden treaty of 1860, all cotton of that description is admitted into France free of duty, if imported in British or French vessels direct from a British port. (*Coton de l'Inde en laine, importé, soit directement des lieux de production, soit des entrepôts du Royaume-Uni sous pavillon Francais ou Britannique.*) American cotton is subject to a duty of 20 francs per 100 kilogrammes or 220 pounds. Previous to 1832 the duty was nearly double that rate when imported in any but French vessels. But by a treaty between France and the United States, concluded that year, the vessels of either country were placed upon the same footing. The importation, however, had to be direct from the place of production, and the origin of the article duly authenticated. A ministerial decree of December 17, 1851, enlarged the provisions of the treaty, so as to extend the equality between the vessels of the two powers, as far as cotton was concerned, even should the American vessel touch at a British port ; but in that event, the captain is required to exhibit a certificate from the French consul at such port, stating that no sale had taken place since it came on board of his ship. This relaxation was doubtless owing to the fact of the steamships of the New York and Havre line, which frequently carried cotton, making Southampton a port of call. The service of those steamers has been discontinued since December 11, 1861 ; but their place has been supplied by German and French lines. The restrictions upon the importations of cotton have been further relaxed, and it is now admitted into the ports of France in the vessels of all nations. The duty on American cotton ought to be removed altogether. The amount generally collected by the French Government, upon its importation, is about 15,000,000 francs. The commerce between the Confederacy and France, since the Cobden treaty came into operation, has been so limited that the injury to the Southern planter, by the discrimination in favor of the Indian ryot, has not yet been seen or felt.

The chief exportations of cotton from Havre are by railway to Switzerland. Next in extent are those to Holland and Sardinia. Smaller shipments are made to the other Italian States, to Spain, and to Austria.

The shipments of cotton yarns and cotton goods from England *to* France, 1858 to 1863 (per British Board of Trade tables), were:

YEARS.		PIECE GOODS.		HOSIERY, LACE, &c.	TWIST AND YARN.	
		Quantity.	Value.	Value.	Quantity.	Value.
		Yards.	£	£	Lbs.	£
1858,	- -	11 566 075	192 432	38 000	800 129	53 393
1859,	- -	9 501 637	174 441	40 000	360 319	33 379
1860,	- -	10 871 407	206 849	41 412	533 931	50 459
1861,	- -	31 331 305	478 327	83 554	1 701 565	187 228
1862,	- -	34 716 448	548 331	190 256	1 890 366	245 807
1863,	- -	30 000 000	455 039	103 991	1 500 000	178 521

The shipments of cotton yarns and cotton goods to England *from* France, 1858 to 1863 (per British Board of Trade tables), in value, were:

			Cotton Manufactures.	Embroidery, &c.
			£	£
1858,	-	-	312 587	21 937
1859,	-	-	371 774	28 658
1860,	-	-	384 251	23 954
1861,	-	-	399 210	25 756
1862,	-	-	450 397	3 552
1863,	-	-	553 602	No returns.

The British Commissioners of Customs, in their report for 1862, give the following account of the working of the Cobden treaty:

France, though not quite coming up to the expectations we expressed last year, as to the extension of her trade in British produce and manufactures, shows, nevertheless, an increase, which must be considered as satisfactory, when the extraordinary impulse given to her dealings with this country in 1861 is remembered. The figures representing the declared value of our exports to that country, are:

1860,	-	-	-	£ 5,249,980	
1861,	-	-	-	8,895,588	
1862,	-	-	-	9,210,523	
Increase in 1861 over 1860,	-	-	-	-	£ 3,645.608
" 1862 " 1861,	-	-	-	-	314,935
" 1862 " 1860,	-	-	-	-	3,960,543

The largest increase is in woolen manufactures. The advance in cotton and linen piece goods, drugs, earthenware and porcelain, is steady and satisfactory, though not equal to that of the former year, even in those articles in which, owing to the reduction of rates in accordance with the treaty, having come the latest into operation, we anticipated last year the largest improvement. In speaking, however, of the results of the treaty, we are justified in taking the two years together, and directing attention to the large increase of £3,960,543.

The demand in this country for the products and manufactures of France, continues to be supplied at an advancing rate, in consequence of the mutual removal of protection duties in both countries by the commercial treaty. While our exports to France shows only an increase of 3½ per cent., the imports from that country, exclusive of corn, grain, and meal of all sorts, which we have omitted in the return, for the reason given in our last report, in the three years, have been as follows:

1860,	-	-	-	£ 13,874,736
1861,	-	-	-	16,658,584
1862,	-	-	-	19,911,903

Showing an increase of 20 per cent. in 1861 over 1860, and a further increase of 19 per cent in 1862 over 1861. The import of cotton manufactures has risen 13 per cent.; of gloves, 13 per cent ; of silk manufactures 8 per cent. ; of woolen manufactures, 18 per cent., and of artificial flowers, 26 per cent."

The commissioners, in their report for 1863, when again speaking of the British commerce with France, remark:

The only foreign country of any importance to which our foreign trade has fallen off, on a comparison with 1862, is our nearest neighbor, France. In the separate return which we have continued this year for that country, as for America, we find the real values for the last five years to be as follows:

1859,	-	-	-	£ 4,754,354
1860.	-	-	-	5,249,980
1861,	-	-	-	8,895,588
1862,	-	-	-	9,209,267
1863,	-	-	-	8,667,138

After the sudden impulse given to our manufactures by the commercial treaty, which threw open a fresh field for trade, and resulted in an increase of 3½ millions in our amount of exports to France for 1861, it is somewhat disappointing to find, first in 1862, as we remarked last year, a less decided rise, and then in 1863 a positive diminution in the demand for our goods. This is to be accounted for partly by the fact that the supply of British goods was at first in excess of the real demand, and partly by the spirit of competition with the English, that has been aroused in the French manufacturer. Prompted by this feeling, he has undoubtedly increased his capital, and set himself with energy to imitate many of our most useful manufactures, which the superior cheapness of labor in his country enables him to do with advantage, and so compete with us successfully in the markets. While, however, we do not for these reasons anticipate any further great extension of our export trade in that direction, we can still look with satisfaction on the increase of nearly four millions in 1863 as compared with 1859, the last year before the conclusion of the commercial treaty.

The commissioners complain that the commerce between the United Kingdom and France, under the new treaty, has not been increased as much as was expected; and in their effort to explain the causes for their disappointment, overlook the fact that since freer trade was established under its provisions, the difficulties in America have arisen. Those difficulties have an indirect bearing upon the trade of England and France, not only with each other, but, as time will demonstrate, with their commerce with the whole world. The partial loss of the American trade to both England and France, has prevented them from receiving the full benefit of the Cobden treaty. Had it not been for that treaty they must have felt the troubles in America keenly. As it is, the treaty stepped in and enabled France and England in a measure to occupy a place towards each other, which was formerly held by the American States. The losses to the nations of Europe, owing to the temporary dethronement of King Cotton, have thus been palliated.

Belgium imports 75,000 bales of cotton of 400 pounds each, one-half of which is the growth of the Southern States; the other half is East Indian cotton, received through England. Her re-exports in the manufactured state amount to one-eighth of all she imports. She buys from England 560,000 pounds of cotton yarn and 3,000,000 yards of cotton goods. The consumption of cotton within her limits is 4 pounds per head. Her population is 5,000,000.

In Spain, the cotton culture and manufacture was introduced by the Moors, and continued by them to some extent for several centuries. The cotton grown in Motril, Kingdom of Granada, was of good staple and much prized. Barcelona was famed for her sail cloth. The cotton sail cloth of the present day, therefore, is no new article of commerce. The fustianeros of Spain wove stout cotton goods, from which the term fustian is derived. Cotton paper was made by the Spanish Arabs. The strong religious hatred that existed between the two rival races on the peninsula, prevented these oriental arts from extending further west, or taking a strong hold on the Christian population, and consequently at the fall of the Saracen empire in Spain, the cotton culture and manufacture relapsed into insignificance. About a quarter of a century ago, the cotton manufacture began to revive, from which time, up to the period of the American war, it had slowly increased. Spain imports annually about 100,000 bales of cotton of 400 lbs. each—80 per cent. of which is the growth of the Southern States. She draws from Brazil about 6,000 bales of the same weight; from Porto Rico, about 700 bales; Cuba, about 300 bales, and the balance from British India via England and the Mediterranean. She also imports about 200,000 pounds of cotton yarn, and 3,500,000 yards cotton goods—the yarns and goods chiefly from England. Her population is 16,500,000. They consume 3 pounds of cotton per head.

Portugal imports about 5,000 bales of cotton annually—nine-tenths of which quantity is received from the Brazils, and the balance is of the growth of the Southern States, obtained through England. Portugal is a large customer to England for cotton yarns and cotton goods—from whom she purchases annually about 300,000 pounds of the one, and 55,000,000 yards of the other. Her population is 3,600,000. The consumption of cotton is at the rate of four pounds per head. The Portuguese, who were the discoverers of the passage to India, via the Cape of Good Hope, made large importations of cotton stuffs and muslins into Europe, but they did not attempt to establish cotton manufactures in their own country.

Cotton was introduced into Italy as a garden plant, at a very early date. It was cultivated as a crop in the eleventh century along the shores of the Gulf of Taranto, where its manufacture sprang up. It was the fashion for the ladies to occupy their spare time in spinning yarn and knitting stockings, which were greatly admired, and sold for high prices. Italian muslins were much in vogue until the end of the last century, when they were superseded by those of India, and in turn by those of England. During the wars of Napoleon the Great, when the "Continental system" was in operation, and cotton could not be obtained from other sources in Europe, Italy produced a considerable quantity of that staple. So much so that the olive tree and the mulberry tree, which at one time were the principal objects of cultivation, were destroyed in order to make room for cotton. This state of affairs existed about ten years. After peace prices of cotton fell so low that cultivation shrank back into its former narrow limits. About 40,000 bales of cotton are now grown in Italy, and she imports a similar quantity—three-fourths of which is of the growth of the Southern States. The Italian States take from England 12,000,000 pounds of cotton yarn and 100,000,000 yards of cotton goods. Italy, in common with all the European countries, held a large reserve of cotton and cotton goods when the "war of the secession" commenced; and under the influence of high prices, she has parted with a large share of her raw material to France and England.

Greece is a grower but not an importer of cotton: nor was she until recently an exporter of that article, in consequence of a heavy duty having been placed upon all cotton leaving her ports   That export duty, which was 40 per cent., has now been reduced to 20 per cent. She is a customer to England for 1,000,000 pounds of cotton yarns and 10,000,000 yards of cotton goods.

The consumption of cotton in Prussia is only about 70,000 bales of 400 pounds each, along with 12,000,000 pounds of yarn and 4,000,000 yards of cotton goods, which she purchases from England.

In Saxony, about 80,000 bales of cotton are consumed by the mills. That quantity is about equally divided between Confederate and East Indian cotton. Saxony is also a large consumer of English yarns.

Bavaria holds an equal position with Saxony towards the cotton trade.

In all the German States, about three pounds of cotton per head are consumed every year by their people. One-half of that quantity is produced by their own mills: the other half is in cotton goods imported from England. The German States are supplied with the cotton consumed in their factories, chiefly through the Hanseatic cities of Hamburg and Bremen. German cotton goods are exported to the American States to the amount of generally 2,000,000 dollars a year. These goods are made principally in Saxony.

Austria hitherto has conducted quite a respectable commerce in cotton with the American States. She has made a pretty rapid stride of recent years in her cotton manufacturing industry She purchases about 170,000 bales of cotton of 400 pounds each—one-third of which reaches her through England, from whom she buys about 5,000,000 pounds of yarn and 20,000,000 of yards of cotton goods. .

The cotton manufactures of Switzerland are known to have existed as early as 1423. In that year a decree was issued by the Canton of Lucerne, directing that cotton goods should be sold by weight. It is conjectured that it is from this decree that the custom originated of selling, entering and clearing cotton goods by weight as well as by measure. The principal cotton marts at that time were France, Germany and Italy. Switzerland manufactures about 75,000 bales of cotton or 30,000,000 pounds per annum. Four-fifths the quantity is imported into Havre, and passed through France by railway, at a heavy expense. The other fifth is obtained through the ports of Germany One-half the cotton used by the mills of Switzerland is of Southern growth. She also imports 2,000,000 pounds of cotton yarn and 30,500,000 yards of cotton goods. The population of Switzerland is 2,500,000, and she consumes within her limits three pounds per inhabitant, or 7,500,000 pounds of cotton a year, and exports in goods, including loss by spinning, 31,000,090 pounds per annum. She ranks next to England, in comparison with her population, in the production of cotton yarns and cotton goods. Her cotton manufactures have largely increased during the last thirty years, without the aid of protective duties, notwithstanding the enormous expense she is subjected to. in obtaining her supplies of the raw material, and sending overland to other countries, the surplus product of her looms. Being situated on the confines of States which impose high protective tariffs on the importation of cotton fabrics, she has pursued the opposite policy, and admitted all goods free of duty. This has caused her people to obtain cheap cotton fabrics, and they therefore have been enabled to smuggle them with advantage into the territories of her neighbors. This contraband trade has yielded large profits. The prosperity of Switzerland is also due to the abundance of her water power, and the great energy, intelligence and industrial genius of her population.

The Dutch, who succeeded in depriving the Portuguese of a portion of their Eastern colonies, imported the cotton goods of India in large quantities, and in the latter part of the sixteenth century established factories of their own to imitate the fabrics of the East. The cotton manufacture has continued to this day. Holland imports about 110,000 bales of cotton of 400 pounds each, three-fourths of which is into Rotterdam, and the remaining fourth into Amsterdam. She likewise imports from England 35,000,000 pounds of cotton yarn and 35,000,000 yards of cotton goods.

Sweden imports 25,000 bales of cotton of 400 pounds each. One-third of her receipts of that staple comes through England, from whom

7

she also purchases 1,000,000 pounds of cotton yarn and 1,200,000 pounds of cotton goods.

Norway imports very little raw cotton. She buys from England 125,000,000 pounds of cotton yarn and upwards of 2,000,000 yards of cotton goods.

Denmark imports from England 2,000,000 pounds of cotton yarn and 3,500,000 yards of cotton cloth.

Russia, previous to the American war, imported upwards of 200,000 bales of cotton a year, about one-third of which was received direct from American ports, and the remainder, with the exception of some small lots of Persian growth, was obtained in England. Russia buys from England about 4,000,000 pounds of yarn and 5,000,000 yards of cotton goods. Russia, like other countries, has been reducing her reserve stock of cotton and cotton goods for several years.

Turkey does not purchase any raw cotton, but she buys annually 25,000,000 pounds of cotton yarn and 300,000,000 yards of cotton goods from England. She exports moderate quantities of raw cotton to Western Europe.

The figures that are given for the cotton trade of the several continental countries, other than France, represent their ordinary commerce. The inflated condition of affairs in connection with that trade, which existed just previous to the American war, will best be seen by statement I, which gives the import, export, consumption and stock of raw cotton in Europe in 1860 and 1861. All the continental markets were likewise largely overstocked with British cotton goods, as the tables of exportations from England for 1860 and 1861 testify. To such an extent was this the case that Russia shipped back to England in 1862, 304,066 pounds of cotton yarn, and Germany returned large quantities of calicoes. Those shipments, which seemed like "sending coals to Newcastle," actually paid handsome profits.

Egypt imports from England about 2,000,000 pounds of cotton yarn and 70,000,000 yards of cotton goods. She is the only country, other than the Confederate States, that exports more cotton in the raw state than she imports in the manufactured condition; and yet she did not commence the cultivation of that staple in earnest until 1818. It seems strange that the two countries that were the latest in engaging in that species of agriculture, should be the only countries that can produce more than they need for their own wants. A great deal of cotton is used in Egypt for making up divans, the usual furniture of the country.

A statement of the cotton trade with British India has been given in the preceding part of this paper.

China takes from England every year about 10,000,000 pounds of cotton yarns and 200,000,000 yards of cotton cloth, as well as 200,000 bales of cotton from India; also from one million and a half to two millions of dollars in value of American cotton goods.

Nearly all the other Eastern countries are customers to England for her cotton fabrics. Africa too is supplied by the looms of Lancashire.

Brazil, as already noticed, sends most of her raw cotton to England; the remainder, with the exception of some little to Spain and Germany, to Portugal. Brazil consumes annually about 140,000,000 yards of British cotton goods, which contain of raw cotton nearly twice the weight of all she exports of that material. Brazil does not import any cotton yarns.

The cotton plant is indigenous to Mexico. Cotton has always been grown there, and manufactures have been conducted on a small scale. Mexico does not export any but Confederate cotton sent thither for reshipment; she is a regular importer of that material to the extent of about 40,000 bales annually for her own consumption. She is likewise an importer of American cotton goods. England usually sends her 200,000 pounds of cotton yarn and 15,000,000 yards of cotton goods.

England is an exporter of cotton goods to all the South American States and to the West Indies. In fact, her cotton fabrics are consumed throughout the world. She exported to the thirty-three States of the late Federal Union, in 1860, 226,776,939 yards of cotton goods, valued at £3,849,915. The quantity was reduced in 1861, owing partly to the secession of the Southern, and partly to the overstocks of goods in the Northern States, to 74,680.537 yards of cotton goods, valued at £1.254,345. In 1862 the figures stood 97,375,709 yards of cotton goods, valued at £1,842,338; and in 1863, (no data) yards, valued at £1,611.835.

When it is considered that 90 per cent. of all the cotton yarns and cotton goods manufactured in England are of Southern cotton, it will readily be seen how important the Confederate States are to her in a commercial point of view. There is no article of commerce that passes through so many hands as cotton—no article of magnitude, in all its ramifications, that employs so much labor. Nor is this all. The cotton of the Southern States, after passing through English machinery, has enabled the British merchants to settle their exchanges with every nation in Christendom. It is not Lancashire alone that is interested in the cotton question. The overthrow of the industry of that locality will act upon the whole country : and that overthrow is inevitable, now that stocks of cotton and cotton goods are reduced, unless cotton can be obtained from the Southern States.

The Northern States of America have prospered under the influence of "King Cotton"—not alone in the manufacture of the staple, which reached as high as 800.000 bales of 400 pounds each, but in many and various ways. New York and New England ship owners earned in latter years over $20,000,000 per annum in carrying cotton to foreign countries and to their own States. They likewise earned large sums in transporting the article when manufactured. The cotton crop was the basis for the settlement of the foreign exchanges of all the States. It gave credit to the North, and was the active promoter of its prosperity. History makes this quite manifest. The Northern States, while colonial dependencies of Great Britain, were only enabled to pay their balances due for importations from Europe by selling their surplus provisions, for which there was no sale on the other side of the Atlantic, to the sister colonies of the West Indies. After the peace of 1783 Great Britain would not permit the "independent" States to trade any more with those islands. The consequence was that the States north of Mason and Dixon's line had no outlet for their produce. All the specie, therefore, that had accumulated during the revolutionary war, by the expenditure of the British and French forces, which found its way into the interior, as well as that received through a commerce clandestinely conducted with the Spanish Main, flowed back to Europe, and those States became impoverished. The Southern States, on the other hand, always had an European outlet for their surplus produce, that kept them out of debt. The Northern States were in a bankrupt condition when the Constitution went into operation in 1789. That very year the French Revolution broke out, and cotton, which had not been much more than a garden plant previously, then assumed for the first time the character of "a crop." The troubles in Europe threw into the hands of the Northern Americans the almost entire carrying trade of the world. That lucrative commerce lasted until the Embargo of 1808, which was placed upon foreign intercourse in retaliation for the Berlin and Milan Decrees of Napoleon, and Orders in Council of England. In the meanwhile, cotton cultivation was expanding, and long before the Peace of Paris (1815,) the Southern States had become the largest cotton exporters of the world; and they continued to hold that position until the Yankee crusade against their rights was commenced. The Federal Constitution received all the credit for the benefits that flowed from the troubles in Europe and the enterprise of the Southern States in extending the cultivation of cotton. Even now the Northern States are dependent upon the Southern States for a supply of cotton. It is a pity that they have been permitted to have a bale. The foolish contracts or "swaps" that have been made with that swapping people (the Yankees) have practically neutralized some of General Lee's brilliant victories. Who ever expected to make any thing by "swapping" with a Yankee? Their smartness in that line of business is proverbial. It is impossible for the cotton mills of the Northern States to do without Southern cotton. They rank next to England as the largest cotton manufacturers. France is third in the list. The total value of cotton goods manufactured in the New England States in 1859 was $~0,301,535, and in the Middle States $26,272,141—an increase of 83.4 per cent. in the former and 77.7 in the latter since the last decade. The other States reached a value of $8,564,280, making the whole production $115,137,926, against $65,501,687 in 1850—an augmentation of 76 per cent. The extension in cotton manufacture was as follows:—Maine and New Jersey, 152 per cent.; Pennsylvania, 102 per cent.; New Hampshire and Connecticut, 87 per cent.; Massachusetts, 69 per cent.; and Rhode Island, 88 per cent. The value was at the rate of $3 69 for each individual in all the States, equivalent to 46½ yards of cloth for every person, at 8 cents per yard. The average production in 1850 was but 34½ yards per head. The increase, therefore, was about 12 yards per individual, or equal to the entire consumption in 1830. The number of hands employed in the manufactories in 1859 was 45,315 males and 73,605 females—an increase of 10,020 and 10,944 respectively over 1850. The average product of an operative was $969, or about £200 sterling. The spindles were returned at 5,035,798, against 3,633,693 in 1850—an advance of 1,402,105, or 38.5 per cent. The cotton manufacturing business of the New England States was 78 6 per cent. of the whole, Massachusetts alone being 29.3 per cent. The product per spindle was—In Maine, $22 12; Massachusetts, $21 12; New Hampshire, $24 87; Vermont, $18 13; Rhode Island, $16; Connecticut, $16 46. The average in the New England States is $20 30; in the Middle States, $30 48; and all the States together, $22 86. The quantity of cotton consumed in the entire Union in 1859 was 364,036,123 pounds; of this amount the New England States took about two-thirds, one-half of which was used in Massachusetts.

The cotton manufacturing business became an important branch of northern industry just after the embargo was placed upon foreign intercourse. The war with Great Britain, that so soon followed, gave it a further start, and it was subsequently pampered by the high tariffs that were placed upon the importation of foreign cotton goods. The Southern States for too long a time allowed themselves to be injured by these protective tariffs, which, although established at first for the purpose of paying off the war debt, operated to the exclusive benefit of the Northern States. The pecuniary loss has been great, but the political misfortunes entailed upon the people of the South has been greater. While that peculiar people (the Yankees) were striking at the peculiar institution of the South, they were absolutely being strengthened by unwise legislation, giving them the benefit of manufacturing nearly one-seventh of the peculiar kind of cotton grown in these States. Yet, in spite of these almost prohibitory tariffs, the importation of cotton goods from Europe into all the States were, for 17 years, in value, as follows :

Year ending June 30, 1845,	-	-	$13,236,830
1846,	-	-	13,360,729
1847,	-	-	12,817,422
1848,	-	-	15,000,000
1849,	-	-	17,205,457
1850,	-	-	15,183,759
1851,	-	-	19,681,612
1852,	-	-	21,486,502
1853,	-	-	18,716,741
1854,	-	-	27,731,313
1855,	-	-	33,949,503
1856,	-	-	21,609,861
1857,	-	-	30,572,352
1858,	-	-	33,128,901
1859,	-	-	20,810,152
1860,	-	-	37,008,232
1861,	-	-	39,615,492

The importations of cotton goods, too, were no doubt largely underinvoiced, to avoid a part of the duties. The very fact of such enormous supplies of cotton goods of foreign manufacture being required, in addition to what was produced in the Northern States, shows the folly of bolstering up a system of cotton manufacturers on this continent. The nations of Europe might with equal propriety continue their futile efforts to grow cotton in other countries. The truth is, America is an agricultural and Europe is a manufacturing continent, and all attempts to change the character of the natural condition of affairs on either side of the Atlantic, must end in political ruin and discomfort. There is a class of cotton goods that are made in the Northern States for exportation to the South American and Asiatic markets. These goods can also be manufactured in the Southern States. They need no protection. England has long since ceased to be a competitor with America in the manufacture of that particular description of fabrics. In Europe it is the habit to separate the qualities of cotton, and either very fine or very inferior goods are the result. American "domestics," however, are made out of good cotton. The grades of the staple are worked up to an average of "middling," and not separated as in England. The reason that the same system is not adopted on both sides of the Atlantic, is, that labor is cheaper in Europe than it is in America. The exportation of American cotton goods began in 1827, and the following figures show the progress of that branch of the cotton trade:

Year	Value	Year	Value
1827,	$1,157,070	1845,	$2,830,550
1828,	1,178,900	1846,	4,427,660
1829,	1,024,299	1847,	3,556,112
1830,	1,289,925	1848,	4,089,480
1831,	1,317,599	1849,	5,695,650
1832,	1,138,675	1850,	4,969,780
1833,	1,239,170	1851,	4,842,930
1834,	2,493,000	1852,	7,396,240
1835,	2,050,940	1853,	7,672,210
1836,	2,831,570	1854,	8,968,900
1837,	2,982,300	1855,	5,535,510
1838,	2,843,700	1856,	5,857,180
1839,	3,686,580	1857,	6,967,310
1840,	3,036,560	1858,	6,111,510
1841,	3,617,080	1859,	5,651,509
1842,	3,161,230	1860,	7,539,532
1843,	3,016,640	1861,	6,816,453
1844,	3,250,080		

The manufacturers of the Northern States have not, by reason of their nearer proximity to the plantations of the South, had much advantage over those of Europe. The expense of sending cotton North is almost as great as that of sending it to Europe. The cry of the American protectionists that cotton was sent, *at a heavy expense*, to be manufactured in Europe, was simply absurd. The cost of transporting raw cotton, and bringing it back in the manufactured state, is very trifling, in comparison with all the other charges entailed upon it. So, while the freights were but little higher to Europe than to New England, the saving in other ways, by making use of the cheaper labor, lower interest and the more suitable climate on the other side of the Atlantic, was very great. After the reopening of the ports of the West Indies in 1830, to American commerce, and the removal of the Federal duty of 3 cents per pound, the North became, to a limited extent, a regular purchaser of cotton from them. The Islands were even nearer to New England than most of the cotton States of the South. The export duty that existed in some of those Islands, lowered the price of the cotton at the place of shipment, and operated, like all export duties on raw produce, as a tax upon the planter. The Northern States have recently been receiving a few thousand bales of inferior cotton from the East Indies. Since the war commenced, the quantity of cotton imported into the Northern States from Europe has been about equal in amount to that which has been exported from the Northern States to Europe. As the quotations on both sides of the Atlantic ascended, a "trapeze" commerce commenced, and the same cotton was several times sent backwards and forwards, until it eventually fell into the lap of the manufacturer. It was, therefore, owing to the tariff system alone, which has been already explained, that the Northern States have been *directly* benefited through the agency of King Cotton, because European countries have had almost equal advantage with them in the purchase of the raw material—particularly since the British import duty was taken off.

But the *indirect* advantages which the Northern States have received through the influence of the commercial monarch, have been manifold. By acting as bankers and commission merchants for the States of the South, those of the North have acquired great credit in Europe, which has enabled them to control likewise the internal commerce of all the States. It has been a mistake to suppose that the Southern States were always largely in debt to the Northern States. At one season of the year—the summer time—when there was no use in the South for money to move the crops, the former became the creditors of the latter. Whenever the balance happened to be the other way, it was not Northern but European capital that was used. The Northerners being a speculative people, have always been "over invested," and the values of their real and personal property since the cotton trade became of importance, have been based upon their commercial intercourse with the South. This was strikingly manifested during the early months of 1861. In the interregnum which existed between the period of the secession of the Southern States, which caused a decline in the internal commerce of "the country," and the large Federal expenditure for the purposes of war, there was a great depreciation in the values of property of every description. That depreciation will again appear, in a much greater degree, after the war expenditure ceases. The North has no cash capital of its own. Ever since the regularity of Atlantic steam communication, the bankers and financiers of Wall street have been borrowers from Lombard street, under a system of floating indebtedness, conducted through the agency of bills of exchange at sixty days' sight. The drafts passing do not as formerly only represent the value of merchandise, but in the numerous ramifications of the money operations, the amount of European acceptances of American bills is probably five or six times greater than the aggregate commercial transactions. This business has been a great source of revenue to New York, the interest charged in Europe being much less than that which is earned in America by reloaning the borrowed capital. The regular commerce between the North and Europe has, in a manner, like the cotton trade of the South, much fallen off. Yet the number and amount of bills of exchange passing between Wall street and Lombard street, is as great as ever. They are accommodation bills chiefly. The machinery of finance thus kept going, while it enables many Anglo-American houses to sustain themselves until "something turns up," likewise benefits the Federal exchequer, as the system of kiting retains British capital on this side of the Atlantic, and prevents the price of gold from ascending. Many of the London-American banking firms must succumb to the storm, whenever Wall street breaks down. One of these "eminent" bankers, Mr. George Peabody, has had the good sense to "clear himself" from danger—he does not even leave his name behind. He has withdrawn from business altogether. It is simply a matter of impossibility for a great war, such as has existed between the American States for nearly four years, not to inflict a blow upon the financial centre of the world; and the longer the conflict lasts, the worse will it be for Lombard street. That financial thoroughfare has been rendered pretty "easy" up to the present time, by the sale of the old stock of cotton and cotton goods—by the conversion of the raw material and manufactured article into cash. England has had more ready money than usual by the sales thus made; but it has been merely turning merchandise into gold and silver—and that gold and silver has been recklessly frittered away.

Englishmen boast of the increase in the value of their exports since the commencement of the American war. They omit to take into account the increased value of their *imports*. The values of both the exports and imports were augmented by the rise in prices of all textile materials, owing to the reduced supply of cotton. The bullion in the Bank of England is a guide as to the course of the foreign exchanges. But the only way to measure the wealth of the United Kingdom in 1865, and to compare it with that of 1860, is to take an account stock of the merchandise on hand, place a value on the same, also to make up a statement of the debts due to England, and place a value upon them. The debtors to England, as a class, are not so solvent as they were in 1860. The Northern States owe her hundreds of millions of dollars, which they never will be able to pay. A little book-keeping will show that the increased prosperity of England these past four years, is nothing more than fiction.

As a specimen of Federal kiting, the following extract from Mr. Fessenden's last report to the Washington Congress is subjoined:

The item of "premium on gold shipped from San Francisco to London" may also require further explanation. In March 1863, it became necessary to transmit a considerable amount of funds to London for a special purpose, for which an appropriation had been made by Congress, and it was thought advisable to deposit a certain amount of our securities with an eminent London banker, against which bills might be drawn. Five-twenty bonds to the amount of $10,000,000 were accordingly passed into the hands of two distinguished citizens, to whose care the negotiation was committed. The negotiation failed, and the $10,000,000 were returned to the Treasury and disposed of. It was thought advisable that the amount of $4,000,000 should remain, and that exchange should be drawn against it, and the bonds disposed of abroad, if a favorable market should be found. It appears, however, that very nearly this amount of issue is in excess of the $511,000,000 authorized by existing loans, $510,756,900 having been disposed of—any bonds known as 5-20's remaining unsold. It is at least questionable whether by this clause power is conferred to dispose of an amount beyond that fixed by existing laws. Additional legislation may remove that doubt, should Congress think it advisable, otherwise they may be canceled. Exchange having been drawn, it became necessary to provide funds to meet the bills at maturity, which was accomplished by shipments of gold from California.

The transaction referred to is only one of the many operations of a similar kind. The Federal Government does not confine its financial affairs to "eminent" firms, but through the Bank of Commerce in New York, an enormous number of bills of exchange are floated upon commercial concerns of less magnitude. Very many millions of dollars have been thrown into Northern coffers by the construction of railways in the North. Very few of those railways ever had much capital stock subscribed. The lenders have been deluded with "bonds;" and so long as the interest is paid upon those bonds—out of the principal of course—"all goes merry as a marriage bell." Pay day, however, will come, when the rottenness of the whole Northern system will be exposed. The Federal railways have had a temporary prosperity occasioned by the closing of the Mississippi to commerce, driving produce North and East instead of South; and by carrying war supplies and soldiers. They, therefore, have been enabled to make flourishing statements to their innocent European bond holders. It is worthy of remark, that the Southern railways, costing some $300,-000,000, have been constructed principally by Southern capital, while those of the North are chiefly owned in Europe. Up to the year 1820 Philadelphia was the financial centre and most important commercial port of the Union; subsequently she became blinded by coal dust; while New York having had the sagacity to increase her trade with the South, took the lead of the former city, notwithstanding she had the formidable influence of the Bank of the United States in her favor. The Erie Canal was not completed until October 26, 1827. A great error has, therefore, been committed, as the dates make manifest, in attributing the rapid advancement of New York altogether to that undertaking, it being quite clear that she progressed by and with the augmentation of the cotton trade. And this fact will be demonstrated when the war expenditure ceases. Trade's "proud empire" will then "haste to swift decay."

The cotton culture has flourished in the Southern States, notwithstanding the pressure of British and Yankee tariffs against it. It is quite clear, that while import duties on *all manufactures* are necessarily paid by the consumers, they, like export duties, when placed upon *raw produce*, come out of the pockets of the agriculturist. It is worthy of remark too, that the only countries who have not aided their cotton manufacturers by a system of protection—England and Switzerland—have prospered more in that species of industry than any others.

The facts presented in this paper should demonstrate the power of "King Cotton." It was impossible for him to exert sufficient influence upon the world, to bring peace to America, so long as there were heavy stocks at all the consuming points; or so long as there was enough cotton leaking through the blockade and through the Federal lines to keep, by mixing with inferior sorts, the mills of neutral powers and the public enemy from coming to a full halt. His importance to England is appreciated only by a few persons. The alarm was sounded some months ago by the accomplished gentleman at the head of the leading financial journal in Europe (the

8

London Economist), a publication noted for its truthfulness. The constant stream of cotton that has been passing out of the South since the article was written, has staved off the apprehended cotton famine. It is on this account that the generality of people, who have neither the time nor the inclination to investigate thoroughly, believe that all the predictions that have been made in reference to American cotton, will prove false. Here is an extract from the article alluded to:

We have pointed out repeatedly that cotton is not cotton in the same sense in which sugar is sugar or tea is tea; that the Indian article or the Egyptian article, however largely furnished to us, could only to a certain extent and in a certain fashion replace the American article; and that we were in great danger of deceiving ourselves, and comforting ourselves prematurely, when we relied on the increase of the number of bales imported or exported from Bombay, or Brazil, or the Levant, as a positive and complete relief from the evils of the cotton famine. Of the long-stapled cotton, such as we still obtain from Egypt, from Pernambuco, and from Maranham, and such as we used to obtain from the small sandy islands lying off the coast of Georgia and the Carolinas, there has never been any lack, and of late there has been a considerable augmentation. Of the very short-stapled cotton, such as India always sent, and such as China, Japan and Syria have begun to send, our supply has increased almost as rapidly and largely on the whole as we could have anticipated. Each of these classes of raw material are adapted for especial uses: the long stapled for muslins, fine and medium yarns, and the *warp* of cloth; the short-stapled, for low yarns and for the *weft* of cloth. But of the moderately short-stapled cotton—such as only North America produces, which is adaptable for almost every purpose, which is immeasurably more valuable than Surat for every case to which Surat is applicable, and which is suited for many uses to which Surat is not applicable, we have been left almost destitute ever since the civil war broke out, and shall remain destitute until the war shall be terminated; and this destitution is, and must continue to be severely felt in Lancashire, how-ver enormous may be the augmentation of our supply of the raw material from other quarters and of other kinds. But this is not all. We have, or at least many of our manufacturers have been too sanguine as to the increased supply from various parts of the world, looking at the supply merely as a gross aggregate, without regard to quality. The amount expected from Egypt was over-estimated; so was that from India. But in reference to this last, there is another consideration. It is true there has been an *apparent* increase. But a large portion of this increase—no one can precisely say *how* large—is apparent only, and is indeed purely deceptive, for this reason. Owing to the enormous prices obtainable, an immense quantity of rubbish has been shipped, under the name of cotton, for which, in ordinary years, no one would have thought it worth while to incur the cost of freight, and which indeed would not have been saleable at *any* price. For example: we know of a recent case in which a manufacturer purchased some Surat at 13d per lb. Not only was it short in ultimate staple, but before this ultimate staple could be arrived at, it had lost 50 per cent in the process—a costly process too—of cleaning—so that the cleaned Indian cotton in reality cost the manufacturer 26d. per lb.—or very nearly the present price of middling New Orleans. Now, the New Orleans would not only have been much more cheaply worked up in all the subsequent processes, and would have been much more willingly, and therefore, in the end, more economically, manipulated by the workmen, but would have produced a decidedly superior article in the end.

China cotton is quite as bad as that of India. A strong dislike has arisen to it, from the great amount of damaged and half-rotten cotton mixed in the bales—the result of putting water into them in China to increase the weight. Most of the lots have, upon landing in England, to be unpacked and made merchantable, at much expense and loss of time, and great difficulties are experienced in settling for arrival and delivery. Smyrna and Turkish cotton generally has sunk in estimation and become very difficult of sale. It is of "wasty" staple, which, with its inflammable nature, makes it better suited for candle-wicks than any thing else. The operatives do not like to work these inferior cottons, in consequence of the large quantity of dirt and "cotton dust" thrown out. That dirt and dust they are obliged to inhale, and it produces disease of the lungs and other maladies. Nearly the whole of the stocks now held in Europe consists of these inferior cottons. Some of the cotton, if ever sold, will not fetch the cost of freight; it is so worthless. Yet every " bale," no matter how small—no matter what kind of cotton it contains—is set down in the published accounts as a " bale" of cotton. Every pound of " rubbish" too that is imported is rated as a " pound" of cotton.

Short-staple cotton, while it answers very well for hand-made goods, will not meet the requirements of machinery, except in very small quantities. As before remarked, the altering of the machinery of some of the mills to spin Surat cotton, proved likewise an advantage in working American cotton. The change in machinery did not of course improve the character of the inferior cotton. A few years before the dissolution of the Federal Union, Mr. J. B. Smith, a member of the House of Commons for Stockport, read a paper before the London Society of Arts, which explained the nature of the kinds of cotton used by British mills. Since the American war commenced, Mr. Smith, as well as all the other members of that body, who favor the Federal cause, has been silent upon the subject, and they will remain silent so long as the Confederacy permits cotton to reach them in sufficient quantities to mix with the poor cottons they obtain from other countries. It has already been explained how the character of British cotton fabrics has deteriorated since the use of inferior cotton in larger proportions than formerly. Here is what Mr. Smith said six years ago:

For practical purposes, and to facilitate the comprehension of the subject by non-professional readers, we may state in general terms that the cotton required for the trade of Great Britain may be classified into three divisions—the long-staple, the medium-staple, and the short-staple.

1 The long staple, or long fibre cotton, is used for making the warp, as it is technically called, i. e. longitudinal threads of the woven tissue. Those threads, when of the finer sorts—for all numbers, say above 50s—must be made of long-staple cotton; for numbers below 50s they may be made of it, and would be so made were it as cheap as the lower qualities of the raw material. No other quality of cotton is strong enough or long enough either to spin into the higher and finer numbers or to sustain the tension and friction to which the threads are exposed in the loom

2 The medium-staple cotton, on the contrary, is used partly for the lower numbers of the warp (and as such enters largely into the production of the vast quantities of ' cotton yarn' and sewing thread exported), but mainly for the weft, or transverse threads of the woven tissue. It is softer and silkier than the quality spoken of above, makes a fuller and rounder thread, and fills up the fabric better. The long-staple article is never used for this purpose, and could not, however cheap, be so used with advantage: it is ordinarily too harsh. For the warp, strength and length of fibre is required; for the weft, softness and fulness. Now, as the lower numbers of ' yarn' require a far larger amount of raw cotton for their production than the higher, and constitute the chief portion (in weight) both of our export and consumption, and as, moreover, every yard of calico or cotton-woven fabric, technically called cloth, is composed of from two to five times as much weft as warp, it is obvious that we need a far larger supply of this peculiar character of cotton, the medium-staple, than of any other.

3. The short-staple cotton is used almost exclusively for weft (except a little taken for candle-wicks), or for the very lowest numbers of warp, say 10s and under, but is different in character from the second description, as well as shorter in fibre; it is drier, fuzzier—more like rough wool; and it cannot be substituted for it without impoverishing the nature of the cloth, and making it, especially after washing or bleaching, look thinner and more meagre; and for the same reason it can only be blended with it with much caution, and in very moderate proportions. But its color is usually good, and its comparative cheapness its great recommendation.

It will be seen, therefore, that while we require for the purposes of our manufactures a limited quantity of the first and third qualities of raw cotton, we need and can consume an almost unlimited supply of the second quality. In this fact lies our real difficulty; for, while several quarters of the world supply the first sort, and India could supply enormous quantities of the third sort, the United States of America alone have hitherto produced the second and most necessary kind.

1. The finest long cotton in the world is called the ' Sea Island.' It is grown on the low-lying lands and small islands on the coast of Georgia. The quantity is small, and the price

very high. It is used mostly for muslin thread, and the very finest numbers of yarn—say 100 and upwards; and price, in fact, is of little moment to the manufacturers who purchase it. It usually sells at about two shillings per pound A quality much resembling it, and almost if not quite as good, has been grown, as a sample article, in Australia. But of this denomination of cotton the consumption is very small. Another species—long, strong, fine, and yellowish—is grown in Egypt, and imported in considerable quantities An inferior quality—coarse, harsh, bright in color, but strong—is imported from Brazil, and a very small quantity from the West Indies. Doubtless if the price were adequate, and the demand here very great and steady, the supply from many of these quarters might be largely augmented. But it is not of this sort that we need any considerable increase, nor could we afford the price which probably alone would remunerate the grower.

2. Our great consumption and demand is for the soft, white, silky, moderately long cotton of America—the quality usually called 'Uplands,' 'Bowed Georgia,' and 'New Orleans.' This used to be sold at prices varying from 3d to 6d per pound (it is now from 6d to 8d); it can be consumed in any quantity, for it is available not only for weft, but for warp, except for the finer numbers. We need and consume nine bags of this cotton for one bag of all other qualities put together.

3. It is the insufficient supply, or the higher price of this cotton, that has driven our manufacturers upon the short-stapled native article of India, called Surat. If the price of the two were equal, scarcely a bag of Surat would be employed. When the price of American cotton rises, owing to an inadequate supply, that of East India cotton follows it at a considerable interval—the usual ratio being two to three—and the import of the latter is greatly stimulated. It is always grown in India in large quantities, and with improved means of communication, and more careful preparation, might be supplied in time in indefinite and probably ample quantities. But it is the quality that is in fault, and, as far as the past is a guide, it would seem incurably in fault. Many attempts to amend the character of this cotton have been made. American planters and American "Saw gins" have been sent over, and American seed has been planted; and the result has been a sensible amelioration in cleanliness and color, and some slight increase in length of fibre, but scarcely any change in specific character. The dry, fuzzy, woolly characteristics remain. Sometimes the first year's samples nearly resemble the American article, but the resemblance never becomes permanent. Hitherto (we believe we are correct in stating), either from the peculiarity of the soil or of the climate, or, as some say, from adulteration by the air-borne pollen of the inferior native plant, the improved and altered character of the cotton has never been kept up.

We are far from saying that this difficulty may not be overcome, and American cotton be naturalized in our East Indian possessions; but certainly the results of our past efforts have not been of favorable augury So far as our own observation and experience have gone, only from two other parts of the world have we seen samples of cotton analogous in character to that of the United States, and equally available for our purposes: one of these was the west coast of Africa, where, we understand, there is a considerable native growth, which doubtless our commerce might encourage and increase; the other is the opposite side of the continent, where Port Natal has exported some very hopeful samples, soft and silky, but not clean nor of a very good color, but still decidedly American in quality.

The point we have to bear in mind, then, is this: our desideratum is not simply more cotton, but more cotton of the same character and price as that now imported from the States. If India were to send us 2,000,000 bales of Surat cotton per annum, the desideratum would not be supplied, and our perilous problem would be still unsolved. We should be almost as dependent on American as ever.

Mr. Smith, in future, will be "far from saying" that the difficulty of "naturalizing" American cotton in the East Indies has been "overcome." He might with almost equal propriety have mentioned Kew Gardens in the neighborhood of London, where specimens of the plant are grown under glass, as a source of supply for cotton, as the other countries which he has named. Further on, in this paper, some important evidence will be adduced in reference to this matter. The idea of "naturalizing" American cotton in India is entirely fallacious, for the very plant that now flourishes vigorously in the Southern States was brought from the Barbadoes, but owing to the change of soil and climate has altered so much from its original stock as almost to deserve the name of another variety. The difference between the soil and climate of the Southern States and India is even greater than that between the Southern States and Barbadoes. While the change to the Southern States benefited the plant, the change to India is known to deteriorate it.

The subjoined table gives particulars of the Southern cotton crops :

The Cotton Crops of the Southern States—1790 to 1860, inclusive.

[The crop is planted and gathered within the calendar year. The exportation is continued to the month of July in the following year. The export column refers to the year in which the cotton was produced.]

YEAR.	Crop.	Price.	Value.	Exported.	Value of Exports.
	Lbs.	Cents.	Dollars.	Lbs.	Dollars.
1790,	1 500 000	30	450 000	189 316	57 000
1791,	2 000 000	29	580 000	138 238	58 000
1792,	3 000 000	26	780 000	500 000	130 000
1793,	5 000 000	35	1 750 000	1 601 760	612 500
1794,	8 000 000	45	3 500 000	6 276 300	2 825 000
1795,	8 000 000	33	2 640 000	6 100 000	2 000 000
1796,	10 000 000	33	3 300 000	3 800 000	1 200 000
1797,	11 000 000	32	3 520 000	9 330 000	3 000 000
1799,	15 000 000	33	4 950 000	9 500 000	3 200 000
1799,	20 000 000	45	9 000 000	17 789 803	8 000 000
1800,	35 000 000	35	8 750 000	20 900 000	7 000 000
	118 500 000	-	39 220 000	76 125 417	25 540 000
1801,	48 000 000	44	21 120 000	27 500 000	12 500 000
1802,	55 000 000	22	12 100 000	41 300 000	9 500 000
1803,	60 000 000	21	12 600 000	38 900 000	8 000 000
1804,	65 000 000	24	15 600 000	40 330 000	10 000 000
1805,	70 000 000	26	18 200 000	37 500 000	9 500 000
1806,	80 000 000	25	20 000 000	66 200 000	16 500 000
1807,	80 000 000	24	19 200 000	12 000 000	3 000 000
1808,	75 000 000	17	12 750 000	53 200 000	9 000 000
1809,	82 000 000	17	13 940 000	93 200 000	16 000 000
1810,	85 000 000	17	14 450 000	62 200 000	10 500 000
	700 000 000	-	159 960 000	472 930 000	104 500 000
1811,	80 000 000	15.50	12 400 000	29 000 000	4 000 000
1812,	75 000 000	9.50	7 125 000	19 000 000	2 000 000
1813,	75 000 000	10.20	7 520 000	17 000 000	1 700 000
1814,	70 000 000	8.25	5 620 000	83 000 000	7 000 000
1815,	100 000 000	20	20 000 000	81 000 000	16 500 000
1816,	124 000 000	30	37 200 000	95 600 000	29 000 000
1817,	130 000 000	24	31 200 000	92 500 000	22 000 000
1818,	125 000 000	30	37 500 000	88 000 000	27 000 000
1819,	167 000 000	25	41 750 000	127 800 000	32 000 000
1820,	160 000 000	16.2	27 000 000	124 893 405	20 157 484
	1 106 000 000	-	227 315 000	757 793 405	161 357 484
1821,	180 000 000	16.6	29 000 000	144 675 095	24 035 058
1822,	210 000 000	11.8	23 500 000	173 723 270	20 445 020
1823,	185 000 000	15.4	28 000 000	142 369 663	21 947 401
1824,	215 000 000	20.9	43 000 000	176 449 907	36 486 649
1825,	225 000 000	12.2	27 000 000	204 535 415	25 025 214
1826,	250 000 000	10	25 000 000	294 310 115	29 359 545
1827,	270 000 000	10.7	28 000 000	210 590 463	22 487 229
1828,	325 000 000	10	32 500 000	264 837 186	26 575 311
1829,	365 000 000	9.9	33 000 000	298 459 102	29 674 883
1830,	350 000 000	9.1	31 500 000	276 979 784	25 289 492
	2 575 000 000	-	300 500 000	2 186 930 000	261 325 802

YEAR.		Crop.	Price.	Value.	Exported.	Value of Exports.
		Lbs.	Cents.	Dollars.	Lbs.	Dollars.
1831,	-	385 000 000	9.8	35 000 000	322 215 122	31 724 682
1832,	-	390 000 000	11.1	42 900 000	324 698 604	36 191 105
1833,	-	445 600 000	12 8	54 000 000	384 717 907	49 448 292
1834,	-	460 000 000	16 8	74 000 000	387 358 992	64 961 302
1835,	-	550 000 000	16.8	88 000 000	423 631 307	71 284 925
1836,	-	570 000 000	14.2	80 000 000	444 211 537	63 240 102
1837,	-	720 000 000	10.3	72 000 000	595 952 297	61 556 811
1838,	-	545 000 000	14.8	76 500 000	413 624 212	61 236 982
1839,	-	871 121 000	8.5	69 760 000	743 941 061	63 870 367
1840,	-	653 978 000	10.2	65 500 000	530 204 100	54 330 341
		5 590 112 000	-	657 600 000	4 570 555 139	557 856 959
1841,	-	673 429 600	8.1	53 850 000	584 717 017	47 593 464
1842,	-	551 550 000	6.2	33 120 000	792 297 106	49 119 806
1843,	-	812 163 600	8.1	65 000 000	663 633 455	54 063 501
1844,	-	957 801 200	5.92	57 500 000	872 905 996	51 739 643
1845,	-	840 214 800	7.81	67 000 000	547 558 055	42 767 341
1846,	-	711 460 400	10.34	71 300 000	527 219 958	53 415 848
1847,	-	939 053 660	7.67	65 775 000	814 274 431	61 998 294
1848,	-	1 091 437 600	6 4	61 620 000	1 026 602 269	66 396 967
1849,	-	838 682 400	11.3	92 300 000	635 381 604	71 984 616
1850,	-	942 102 800	12.11	113 050 000	927 237 089	112 315 317
		8 357 896 000	-	680 515 000	7 391 826 980	611 394 797
1851,	-	1 296 011 600	8.05	96 500 000	1 093 230 689	87 965 732
1852,	-	1 305 152 800	9.85	130 000 000	1 111 570 370	109 456 404
1853,	-	1 172 010 800	9.47	111 350 000	987 833 106	93 596 220
1854,	-	1 138 935 600	8 74	99 650 000	1 008 424 601	88 143 844
1855,	-	1 411 138 000	9.49	141 100 000	1 351 431 701	128 382 802
1856,	-	1 175 807 600	12.55	147 000 000	1 018 282 475	131 575 859
1857,	-	1 245 584 800	11.70	146 300 000	1 118 624 012	131 386 661
1858,	-	1 606 600 000	11.75	188 700 000	1 372 755 006	161 434 923
1859,	-	2 078 777 000	10.85	228 690 000	1 767 686 338	191 806 555
1860,	-	1 645 238 700	11 07	181 500 000	1 407 405 600	155 000 000
		13 985 456 900	-	1 470 790 000	12 267 243 848	1 278 748 549

Recapitulation.

DATE.		Crops.	Value.	Exported.	Value of Exp'ts.
		Lbs.	Dollars.	Lbs.	Dollars
1790 to 1800,	-	118 560 000	39 220 000	76 125 417	25 540 000
1801 to 1810,	-	700 600 000	159 960 000	472 930 000	104 560 000
1811 to 1820,	-	1 103 000 000	227 315 000	757 793 405	161 357 484
1821 to 1830,	-	2 575 000 000	300 500 000	2 186 930 000	261 325 802
1831 to 1840,	-	5 590 112 000	657 600 000	4 570 555 139	557 856 959
1841 to 1850,	-	8 357 896 000	680 515 000	7 391 826 980	611 394 797
1851 to 1860,	-	13 985 456 900	1 470 790 000	12 267 243 848	1 278 748 549
		32 432 964 900	3 536 100 000	27 723 404 789	3 000 723 521

It will be seen by the above table, that six-sevenths of all the cotton that has been grown in the Southern States was exported to foreign countries, and that the remaining one-seventh has been consumed in the States of production and the more Northern States of the late Federal Union. . The average quantity of cotton consumed each year by the inhabitants of all the States, North and South, was 12 pounds per head. Of that quantity, the greater proportion was consumed in the Southern States. Very little economy has hitherto been practiced in the use of raw cotton in those States. It was so plenty on the plantations and so cheap in the home markets, that much was wasted every year. As prices are likely to rule high for some time to come, it will be well if in future more care is taken of the staple. The Southern States before the war were large importers of European and Yankee textile fabrics of all kinds. Being in a measure cut off from the usual supplies, and not being cultivators of flax or wool to any great extent, they have been compelled to use cotton goods as a substitute for those manufactured from other materials. The quantity of cotton consumed in the place of leather must also be very great, not to speak of that required for tents, wagon covers, and the like. The home consumption then, of raw cotton, must come up to 50,000 bales a month, or 600,000 bales per annum, to say nothing of the wastage that is going on at a rapid rate. Cotton is not a perishable article when properly baled and stored in warehouse; but when not taken care of, it speedily damages, deteriorates in quality, and loses in weight prodigiously. The table includes the growth and exportation of Sea Island cotton. The seed for that description of cotton was introduced from the Bahamas in 1785, and its culture has been greatly improved by "naturalization." The crops do not increase in extent; they were nearly as large in the early part of the century as they were in 1 60. The annual yield is about 12,000.000 pounds; which is fully equal to the demand.

It is now only ninety-two years since fabrics made entirely of cotton were first manufactured in England. At that time—177: —the raw material was imported to the extent of about 4,000,000 pounds weight a year from the West Indies and the Mediterranean. The Southern States contributed their first supply in 1784, when eight bags were exported from Charleston to Liverpool. They were seized by the custom house authorities there, under the belief that they were of colonial growth, and that their importation was, therefore, in violation of the then existing navigation laws. They were released so soon as it was ascertained that cotton could be grown in the Southern States. There had been exported from Charleston in 1748, 7 bags, and in 1770, 10 bags of cotton. These two invoices were probably of island growth; at all events they attracted no attention, as South Carolina was, when the shipments were made, a dependency of Great Britain. With the exception of the 100,0 0 pounds of Indian cotton, received v a Ostend in 1757, the first supply of Surats was landed in England in 1795. England had hitherto been an importer of cotton yarn as well as piece goods from India. The increase afterwards in her cotton trade will be seen by the following table:

British Imports of Raw Cotton, 1800 to 1863.

[In the second and third columns of this table three figures are omitted on the right hand, so that millions of pounds weight read as thousands.]

YEARS.	Col. 2. Imported into the United Kingdom.	Col. 3. Imported from the Southern States.	YEARS.	Col. 2. Imported into the United Kingdom.	Col. 3. Imported from the Southern States.
1801.	55 675	18 953	1833.	303 656	237 506
1802,	60 289	23 473	1834,	326 875	269 203
1803,	53 427	27 757	1835,	363 702	284 455
1804.	61 316	25 770	1836,	406 959	289 615
1805,	59 649	32 661	1837,	407 286	320 651
1806,	57 982	24 255	1838,	507 850	431 437
1807,	74 786	53 180	1839,	389 396	311 597
1808,	43 263	7 992	1840,	592 488	487 856
1809,	91 701	13 365	1841,	487 992	358 240
1810,	134 805	36 171	1842,	531 750	414 030
1811,	91 908	46 772	1843,	673 193	574 738
1812,	61 563	26 086	1844,	646 111	517 218
1813,	~	-	1845,	721 979	626 650
1814,	52 887	-	1846,	467 856	401 949
1815,	98 790	45 669	1847,	474 707	364 599
1816,	93 685	57 793	1848,	713 020	600 247
1817,	124 303	52 668	1849,	755 469	634 504
1818,	177 178	65 985	1850,	663 576	493 153
1819,	149 467	63 675	1851,	757 379	596 638
1820,	149 322	89 999	1852,	929 782	765 630
1821,	132 536	93 470	1853,	895 278	658 451
1822,	142 837	101 131	1854,	887 333	722 151
1823,	191 402	142 532	1855,	891 702	681 629
1824,	149 380	92 187	1856,	1 023 886	780 040
1825,	228 005	139 908	1857,	969 319	654 758
1826,	177 607	130 858	1858,	1 034 342	833 238
1827,	272 448	216 924	1859,	1 225 989	961 707
1828,	227 760	151 752	1860,	1 390 939	1 115 891
1829,	222 767	157 187	1861,	1 256 985	830 000
1830,	263 961	210 885	1862,	523 973	34 042
1831,	288 674	219 333	1863,	669 583	61 743
1832,	286 832	219 756			

The exportations of raw cotton from the United Kingdom to Continental Europe, are chiefly of East Indian sorts, which can be used there as in England, in small portions, with that of the growth of the Southern States. It is the use of American cotton that creates a demand for Indian cotton. So, without the American staple the British trade with India must diminish—shrink back to its former limited extent. It has already been stated that the chief exports to India are of Manchester goods made out of American cotton. A period, therefore, is sure to be reached when both the import and export trade between Great Britain and India will be of small moment, unless a sufficient quantity of the raw material is again contributed by the Southern States. England has already parted with her enormous stocks of cotton goods made from good cotton. Their sale has placed her in specie funds. These funds she has, in a great measure, foolishly squandered in the East in buying an inferior staple, and in the hope of opening up new sources of supply for cotton. The gold and silver thus transferred will never be returned to her. It is well known that the ryots in India and the fellahs in Egypt bury their money. They not only like to hide their wealth from fear of their governments placing additional burdens upon them in the way of taxation, but it has always been a custom among them so to do. That feeling of dislike to parting with gold and silver is not confined to the inhabitants of the East. It exists on the Western Continent. It would have been much better for the people of these States, if every ounce of gold had been sent to Europe and the North to purchase supplies, than that cotton should have been sent out so lavishly these past eighteen months.

The sources of the British cotton supply, at the time when the manufacture of that staple was beginning to assume dimensions of national importance, were the British, French, Spanish, Dutch and Portuguese colonies, which furnished three-fourths the entire quantity. In all these colonies agricultural labor was performed by slaves exclusively. The very small quantity then obtained from the East Indies, through Ostend, may be altogether disregarded. And the remainder—less than one-fourth of the whole—received from Smyrna and Turkey, can scarcely be set down as the fruit of free labor. The relative per centage of each source of supply soon afterwards changed. Of the entire quantity of cotton imported into Great Britain in 1824, the Southern States, Brazil and the West Indies, all using only slave labor, furnished 79 per cent. Turkey and Egypt, 6½ per cent. The East Indies, 9 per cent.; and other countries about 5 per cent. Subsequently, the Southern States increased their portion to 85 per cent., and supplied the Continent of Europe and the Northern States with most of their cotton. It is a fact that there is not, and never has been any considerable source of supply for cotton, excepting the East Indies, which is not obviously and exclusively maintained by slave labor. The value of the exception is of little moment, and of still less importance when it is considered that the condition of the ryot does not appear to be such as to impart to his operations, either as a laborer for hire, or as an independent cotton grower, the productive advantages that are associated with free labor. He is, in fact, elevated but little above a slave.

On August 13th, 1862, there was held in London a conference between a deputation from the Cotton Supply Association and the "Commissioners and other representatives of countries showing raw cotton in the International Exhibition." As very little publicity was given to the proceedings, a few extracts from the report printed for private circulation, may not be out of place. Mr. J. Cheetham, the Chairman, said:

It does so happen, gentlemen, at this precise moment, when the representatives of industry, and of capital, and of enterprise from every part of the world are gathered together in this country, that, as regards the great leading manufacture—the one upon which the prosperity, and to a great extent, the greatness of England depends—it does so happen that this staple and leading manufacture is at the present moment in a position unexampled in its history, and one, the prospect of which I, as an individual, look forward to for the next few months with feelings of the deepest anxiety, if not of despair. You are aware, gentlemen, that this state of things has been brought about by the civil war in America.

9

America has been the main supplier of cotton to the industrious operatives not only of England, but of the whole world, and the present position in which the cotton cultivation of that country is placed—though expected at some more distant time to have arisen from an insurrection of the slaves—has unexpectedly been occasioned by dispute and animosity among Americans themselves.

Mr. Stephen Cave, M. P., an abolitionist, and the only member of the House of Commons who has had the candor to declare that "while there has been a great change in English opinion on the subject of slavery, he believes that there is yet no Englishmen in favor of reopening the African slave trade," was one of the speakers. Mr. Cave represented the West India interest at the Cotton Conference. He said :

I have taken some pains in looking through the accounts of former years, and I find that the whole produce of all the West Indies was from ten to twelve millions of pounds of cotton. That is a very small quantity, of course, compared with the whole import of some thousands of millions of pounds, which is the present import of cotton into this country; but in those days it was considered of more importance than at present it appears to be. With regard to the future, I can only echo what has been stated by my friend, Mr. Marsh, that price and labor are the two elements which we are to look to in this question. There is no doubt that every island in the West Indies can grow cotton perfectly well. The Grenadines, a group of small islands off the coast of St. Vincent, of which that is the principal, grew most excellent Sea Island cotton. At the time of the emancipation, negroes who grew that cotton got tired of living on small patches of land, and they went off to the neighboring island of St. Vincent for society, and the production of cotton was almost entirely given up in the other colonies, for the same reason that we were brought more rapidly into competition with slave grown cotton than with slave grown sugar; consequently, sugar paid better for a longer period in the West Indies than cotton did. We know that sugar does not pay very well now, and therefore the people of that country are quite willing to turn their attention to any thing which they imagine will give them a better return for their capital than sugar does at the present moment. Now the colony of British Guiana was the one which produced the largest quantity of cotton in former days. I may dismiss Barbadoes at once, because, although labor is abundant in Barbadoes, and cotton could be grown in Barbadoes to pay, yet, in consequence of the excellence of the soil for the production of sugar, I do not think it likely that the cultivation of the sugar will be given up for the cultivation of cotton, and there is not enough land for both. But in British Guiana there is any amount of unoccupied land; there is also a rail road there, and at the end of that railway there is a quantity of land—and my friend, Sir William Holmes, will confirm my testimony—which is available for growing, if not the best cotton, at any rate the quality of cotton that this country wants most—the ordinary Orleans cotton. The question is, how is that to be grown ? I have but little doubt that the present population of British Guiana is totally inefficient for such a purpose, and negro labor cannot be relied on. We have heard a great deal about a cotton company which has lately been established in Jamaica, and we have had favorable reports with regard to it. I have no doubt these reports are perfectly correct, and I only hope we shall have the same kind of reports for a year to come ; but I must say this with regard to the cotton company, it is a new thing, and one knows that negroes will turn with great eagerness to any thing new, but after a time they get tired of it, and give it up for something else. Besides that, we must remember that a very large number of sugar estates have been abandoned in Jamaica, and there is no doubt, therefore, that there is a large amount of available unoccupied negro labor. If there were a large number of cotton companies established in that country, there would be the same difficulty in regard to the labor that there was in regard to the cultivation of sugar, which caused those estates to be abandoned, we think it comes to this, we must import labor. * * * I need not say it is not the rate of wages so much as the *command* of labor, that is of great consequence in these things. A very low rate of wages may ruin a man, if he cannot command a constant supply, whereas a high rate of wages may make him rich, if he can command it.

Mr. Ridgway, a representative from Jamaica, said :

I am also somewhat concerned for British Guiana ; but inasmuch as I stand in rather an equivocal position in that quarter, I will not say much upon it, except that in former years British Guiana was a very great cotton growing country. I have in my hand a return showing that in the ten years from 1834 to 1844, there was an immense falling off. Why ? Because of the difficulty of obtaining help, and because a higher price could be got for raising sugar than for raising cotton. In the year 1834 there were 2,188 bales exported from Demarara and Essequibo, and 1,188 from Berbice, making a total in that year of 3,376 bales. Well, in the course of ten years it has dwindled down, till in 1843 there were

6 bales from Demarara and Essequibo, and 16 from Berbice—making a total of 24 bales. In the year 1844 there was not a single bale exported. Now that arises mainly from very great mistakes that people make in not considering questions of vital importance Here were certain gentlemen who were desirous of doing away with the slave trade, and of suppressing negro cultivation. If they had reflected properly, as they ought to have done, they would have seen that the course of proceeding, though very kindly intended, was very prejudicial to the people themselves, as well as to the mercantile community, especially in relation to this cotton question. Now, what we want in the West Indies, in Jamaica, and British Guiana, is labor.

Mr. Kendall, the representative from Peru, said:

The seed in Peru is put into the ground by hands, so that when a plantation, say of six miles in breadth is sowed, it may well be believed that a large capital is required to pay the laborers. This is sensibly felt now that slavery is no longer in use in the republic. Slavery was then abolished during the last revolution; and although humanity has been a great gainer, agriculturists are no small losers by the operation. I have been assured by Mr. Quiretaua, that when Mr Elias had 700 negroes in his establishments, and one-half of them were employed in cultivating cotton, his crops produced from 14,000 to 20,000 quintals; whilst at the present time he can scarcely get in 10 or 12,000 quintals—the remainder being lost through want of hands. As bearing upon this subject, it may be here related that in former years Mr. Elias was actually accustomed to purchase cotton of his own producing. For instance, when the daily amount of labor allotted to each negro was over, he would pay them a shilling for every 25 lbs. of cotton they brought in, as being gathered during the time which was set apart for the rest and recreation of the slave.

The Mauritius is in the same condition in respect to labor. Mr. James Morris, the representative from that "possession," said:

Mauritius has sent a small specimen of its cotton to the Exhibition, more as a botanical than as a mercantile specimen. Formerly the Mauritius was remarkable for the beauty of its cotton. In connection with its sister Island—Bourbon—it exported to France a very large amount of cotton, being then a French Colony. In 1790 its export was 300,000 bales. At the present moment, like the Barbadoes and other West Indian Colonies, the cultivation of sugar has displaced the cultivation of cotton.

Mr. Simmonds, who represented Siam and Dominica, said:

It seems to me, that our South African Colonies have not been spoken to at all. I do not see Mr. Sergeant here, the representative of Natal. It is a cotton producing country, and it might be made a cotton producing country to a much greater extent, I think. We have specimens in the exhibition of the cotton of that Colony: labor is very plentiful there, and what has been the reason of the failure of an ample supply of cotton? It is owing to the uncertainty of labor which is to be obtained from any savage tribe. The same difficulty arises in the West Indies. We cannot get a continuous labor from the African race, whether in a barbarous or more civilized country; you cannot indoctrinate in them those civilized wants which European races, and especially the Anglo-Saxon races exhibit. Where a climate produces food so abundantly as those climates do, and clothing is almost unnecessary, the people will not work continuously; they will only work by fits and starts, and that is the great difficulty you have to overcome in those countries. I believe that Natal and parts of South Africa would produce cotton to a very considerable extent. They are endeavoring there to introduce laborers as the Mauritius has done, by bringing Coolies from India. If we could glance over most of those colonies which we have seen producing cotton in the Exhibition, we should see that a great deal could be done if the question of labor could be got over—that serious point which has been already adverted to by so many gentlemen. It of course affects Dominica, of which I am a representative. There are, for instance, the Bahamas, where a great deal of cotton might be produced. They formerly produced a great deal of fine cotton, and they now produce, in many of their out-lying islands, pine apples, which certainly do not pay as well as cotton would if it were to be cultivated. The question is, where can you get your labor?

Mr. Walker, from the West Coast of Africa, said:

As I have been called upon, I beg to offer a few remarks, and I think, as a resident of upwards of eleven years on the West Coast of Africa, I have a right to speak upon the subject. I have carried on an extensive business in the Gaboon and the neighborhood for the last eleven years, and I certainly must say from my experience, although I know well small quantities of cotton have been produced under the superintendence of Mr. Lecompte and other gentlemen privately, as samples, and very good samples, that it is quite out of the question, and utterly impossible, for many years to come, that any quantity of cotton of importance to commerce could be produced on the West Coast of Africa. I am perfectly certain, that with the exception of Aberkúta, and Lagos, and the Niga, which are the only points on the coast of Africa capable of shipping cotton in a state to be of marketable value on its arrival in England, that there is not the slightest chance for many years to come, of any cotton being exported from those countries, except to a homœopathic and infinitesimal extent. The difficulties in the way of shipment, and the dearness of labor, are all great obstacles to the cultivation of cotton in, and its exportation from the West Coast of Africa.

Mr. Ridgway, who volunteered in behalf of Natal, said:

As there was nobody present, to represent Natal, the Cape of Good Hope and the East Coast of Africa, he would venture to say that the productions of Natal, as shown in the present Exhibition, were astonishing. There was a variety of most valuable products—useful in every kind of way; and among them there was nothing perhaps so important as the article of cotton. The people of Natal were exerting themselves in every direction to produce cotton abundantly and of good quality, and in a manner creditable to go into the Manchester market. The difficulty they have in Natal is to get emigrants from Europe.

There were a small number of Hottentots, and all sorts of nations of Africa, in that part of the coast, who were willing to work; but there was a very fierce and troublesome set of people, in the shape of Caffres, and other tribes. Fortunately there were missionaries now among them, who were quieting them and bringing them to think how they might live honestly and peaceably by their industry.

This question of labor is a most important one, as far as cotton cultivation is concerned. It will be observed how freely the gentlemen of the International Exhibition spoke about it. The abolitionism of England was no doubt sincere as long as it lasted—over a quarter of a century—but it is now vanishing. The statesmen of the present day see the blunder that was committed by the passage of the Emancipation measures. Those measures originated out of a purely philanthropic feeling, which amounted to a furore. While it was vainly imagined that the negro was being benefited, it was also thought that free labor would be cheaper than slave labor, and that in the end the £20,000,000 sterling paid for the purchase of the slaves, would be returned to the British community in the shape of cheaper produce. The Emancipation act was therefore passed under the influence of a double set of views. It was not adopted, as is supposed by many persons, for the purpose of building up the East Indies to the detriment of the West Indies. Nor was it adopted with a view of breaking down American institutions. Neither was the fanaticism that followed in any degree induced with that wish. Happily, a great change has taken place in the minds of the British people in respect to slavery. That change had commenced to take place before the disruption of the American States; and the chief fear that Englishmen had prior to that event, was, that there would be an insurrection among the slaves at some time, and that in such case they would be deprived of their customary supplies of cotton from the Southern States. Like the protectionists and abolitionists of the Northern States, the cotton lords with those in their interest joined hands, and made an effort to seek new sources of supply, so as to be prepared for such a contingency as the stoppage of receipts from the Southern States. At the time abolitionism was started in England, the cotton manufacturing industry of the Kingdom had not assumed such important dimensions as when the war in America occurred. It is therefore absurd to suppose that abolitionism was established for the purpose of making a direct blow at the cultivation of cotton in the Southern States. Horrible as this war has been, it will not prove an unmixed evil, for it will demonstrate to the other powers of the world their dependence upon the fibre of these States. It has been the enormous stocks of raw cotton and cotton goods made from the products of the Southern States, with the quantity of cotton that has eluded the blockade, and been " swapped" to, and stolen by the Yankees, that has caused the neutral powers to be passive viewers of the American contest. For the same reasons there has not been any " cotton famine" yet. The "operatives" were overemployed before the war, and since the conflict they have been underemployed.

The writer stated in another part of this paper that the Manchester manufacturers had been deceiving their neighbors, by making "a poor mouth;" that by such means they had received from other classes of the community aid in the support of their idle operatives. He also stated that the parties interested in the cotton trade at one time did not desire the war brought to a close, and that when the British Government entertained the idea of recognizing the independence of the South, those parties objected to such a movement. The writer was an eye witness to this procedure, and took upon himself to say in the English newspapers, that the South could not " deluge" Manchester with cotton after the loss of one crop, and the partial destruction and wastage of another. At that time, when all Confederates in Europe had hoped, indeed fully expected British action in the affairs of their country, the conference committee from the Cotton Supply Association and the representatives of the petty cotton growing countries, held the meeting above alluded to. Mr. Hugh Mason of Lancashire, a very influential member of the Association, made a speech on that occasion, and in his remarks appear the following words:

Having said so much about India, just allow me at the same time to say one or two words in reply to the representative from Ecuador, who, perhaps, somewhat deservedly re proached the Lancashire men for not having come forward more earnestly with their capital in aid of the various new cotton schemes which have been from time to time launched by various individuals. Now, upon that point, allow me to say that something is to be said for Lancashire men. Lancashire men, like other men, have worked hard for their money, and, having earned that money, *they do not wish to lose it at a time like this*, when they see their capital daily and hourly getting smaller and smaller. Now, they have been terrified by that bugbear, that there are four millions of bales of American cotton at this moment shut up; that, perhaps any mail might bring the news that a peace had been patched up in America; that the quarrel had been compromised, and that their four million bales of cotton would be let loose upon Lancashire like a deluge. Now, I need only ask gentlemen of common sense, men of business, what would be the position of things if such an event were to happen? Would not a great many of the cotton schemes which have been launched be at once knocked in the head? I cannot, therefore, blame the cotton spinners for having shown a degree of caution and reserve in taking up with new enterprises of a kind so foreign to their habits and pursuits. *I am also prepared to deprecate very earnestly indeed the language which has been used by men in high official position in this country, with respect to the prospect of the duration of this war. Earl Russell little knows the mischief he did in Lancashire; the loss he was the means of inflicting upon the Lancashire cotton spinners, by that statement which he made a few months ago in Parliament, when he gave it as his opinion that the war would be terminated in ninety days.* I am prepared to say, gentlemen, that I know orders were not given out that would have been given out, and orders withdrawn that had been given, in consequence of that statement, and the price of yarns and cloth were considerably reduced in consequence. *A statement of that kind caused a great amount of mischief and a great amount of consternation in Lancashire.*

The reasons that caused the people of Lancashire in 1862 to protest against the British Government lending its assistance, morally or otherwise, towards bringing about peace in America, have long since vanished. Those very people would no doubt ere this have urged the Ministry to renew their intention of doing justice to the South, had they not been supplied with sufficient cotton from the Confederacy to make a good "mix" with the inferior sorts received from other countries. The slavery question has not influenced in any degree the course of the rulers of England. They know perfectly well that cotton cannot be cultivated by free negro labor; that the cotton plant is so delicate in its nature, that its cultivation cannot be left to the caprice of free black "operatives." The writer goes so far as to say, that if the statesmen of England became satisfied that there was an insufficiency of slave labor in the South to work the cotton fields after the cessation of hostilities, they would not stand in the way of the planters obtaining "help" of the right kind, even if from Africa. A supply of good cotton will, after the lapse of some months, be of vital importance to Great Britain—of much more consequence than most people think.

England cannot afford to do without American cotton. No species of industry can possibly take its place. So long as all the parties interested in the cotton trade were making money by the stoppage of the usual supplies of cotton, they were contented to partially support their idle operatives. Those operatives, be it remembered, had been fully employed at high wages for several years before the war, and had saved large sums (for them) of money, which they had invested in the savings banks. They now, however, have expended all their former earnings, sold their surplus furniture, and their demands, upon the public will therefore be larger than hitherto. Unless England obtains a full supply of American cotton, there will be a revolution—a civil war—in the British Isles. It was the vast extension of the cotton trade that enabled England to throw open her ports for grain at a fixed duty of one shilling per quarter instead of the old sliding scale. She has yet plenty of soil uncultivated. If the persons directly and indirectly engaged in the manufacture of cotton, are permanently thrown out of their accustomed employment, they will have to become tillers of that soil. In which event, the yield of wheat will be augmented, and importations of grain will have to be checked by a renewal of the sliding scale, or her agricultural interests will be ruined. Situated commercially as England is, if she produced from her soil as much as she did previously to 1845—sometimes nearly enough cereals for her own consumption—she could not permit herself to be subjected to the risk of an avalanche of breadstuffs falling upon her, when there happened to be a large overproduction in other countries. The very danger of such a contingency would materially affect the value of her landed property, and upset her whole political system. But so long as England, Wales, Scotland and Ireland only grow enough grain to last them for nine months in the year, they can readily have open ports to receive the other three months' supply, or about 40,000,000 bushels of wheat, to say nothing of Indian corn. It was not Mr. Cobden nor Mr. Bright that caused the repeal of the British corn laws. It was the great development of the

British cotton trade, which took place just about the time of the Irish famine.

With the exception of the period just previous to the fall of Fort Sumter, the stocks of *raw cotton* in England were greater in 1845 than they have been at any other time, and prices for New Orleans middling fell below 3½d per pound. The duty of 5-16ths of a penny per pound, or 2s 11d per cwt., was taken off; and as the quantities of cotton goods at the consuming points were then of moderate extent, the trade took a sudden start, became very prosperous, and many persons who had been employed in agricultural labor, assumed the character of operatives. The Irish famine occurred the following year (1846), and the corn laws were temporarily repealed. In another season the cotton trade had so expanded that it became more profitable to manufacture that staple than to force agriculture. The sliding scale was then permanently set aside; and since that time the British community has expended in the purchase of food in other countries, about £20,000,000 per annum. The writer, though a free trader, frankly admits that the sliding scale of duties operated to the advantage of England as long as they were in existence. Wheat, unlike cotton, is a perishable article, and cannot be retained beyond a certain length of time. It has to be sold. England, therefore, with her ships visiting all the grain growing countries, had to establish measures by which she would not be liable to a flood of grain. Those measures were rescinded so soon as there became, by reason of her cotton manufacturing industry, no danger of her being thus flooded. Since the vast enlargement of the cotton trade, the wealth of Great Britain, in point of distribution, is relatively less in real estate than before that period. The enormous amounts represented in railways, steam ships and other enterprises since the repeal of the corn laws, have greatly changed the character of British home investments. The prosperity of those enterprises, too, depends upon the continuance of her commerce in cotton. So, look at it as we may, it is a matter of impossibility for Great Britain to retain her present pre-eminent position without the yield of Southern soil.

[A.]

A Statement showing the stocks and value of Raw Cotton in warehouse on the 1st of January of each year, and the quantity and value imported into and exported from Great Britain and Ireland in the six years, 1858 to 1863.

Years.	Stocks and value of cotton in warehouse on the 1st January each year.			Imported during the year.	Exported during the year.	Excess of imports.	Yarn producing properties of excess of imports.	Average price of cotton.	Value of imports.	Value of exports.	Net cost of cotton.
	Weight.	Yarn producing properties.	Value.								
	Lbs.	Lbs.	£	Lbs.	Lbs.	Lbs.	Lbs	Pence.	£	£	£
1858	182 361 530	155 007 301	4 943 125	1 034 342 176	149 609 600	884 732 576	752 022 691	7	30 106 968	3 955 309	26 151 659
1859	113 959 620	96 865 677	2 967 698	1 225 989 072	175 143 136	1 050 845 936	893 219 047	6¾	34 559 636	4 218 390	30 341 246
1860	197 663 710	168 014 154	4 941 593	1 390 938 752	250 428 640	1 140 510 112	969 433 535	6 3-16	35 756 889	5 388 190	30 368 699
1861	250 286 605	206 486 450	7 300 026	1 256 984 736	298 287 920	958 696 816	790 924 875	7¾	38 653 398	8 577 747	30 075 651
1862	291 674 450	218 755 837	13 368 412	523 973 296	214 714 528	309 258 768	231 951 576	14½	31 093 045	13 508 601	17 584 444
1863	161 561 870	107 041 247	13 463 490	669 583 264	241 750 992	427 832 272	285 221 515	20¼	56 277 953	20 145 916	36 132 037
1864	123 644 785	74 186 871	12 364 478								
				6 101 911 296	1 329 931 816	4 771 876 480	3 922 773 299	–	226 447 889	55 794 153	170 653 736

[B.]

A Statement showing the quantity and value of the Cotton Yarns and Cotton Goods imported into the United Kingdom of Great Britain and Ireland, and the Foreign Cotton Manufactures exported therefrom during the years 1858 to 1863.

YEARS.	Cotton yarns imported.		Value of cotton piece goods imported.			Total value of yarns and goods imported.	Cotton yarns re-exported.		Value of cotton goods re-exported.	Total value of yarns and goods re-exported.	Excess in value of imports over exports.	Weight of yarns and goods imported and exported. Imported in the six years, 65,000,000 lbs. Exported in the six years, 13,000,000 lbs.
	Weight.	Value.	From India and China.	From Continental Europe.	Total.		Weight.	Value.				
	Lbs.	£	£	£	£	£	Lbs.	£	£	£	£	lbs.
1858,	799 827	85 045	71 279	502 944	574 223	659 268	321 167	38 381	115 061	153 442	505 826	
1859,	962 097	112 151	39 921	642 079	682 900	795 051	648 668	77 947	117 567	195 514	599 537	
1860,	1 002 872	112 901	72 971	685 059	758 030	870 931	797 934	96 802	138 934	235 736	635 195	
1861,	1 005 174	121 684	130 561	652 482	783 043	904 727	568 535	65 405	140 078	205 483	699 244	
1862,	1 246 748	126 059	158 215	741 523	899 738	1 025 797	476 162	53 002	175 609	228 701	797 096	
1863,	1 100 000	150 000	134 904	900 000	1 034 904	1 184 904	400 000	50 000	200 320	250 320	934 584	
	6 116 718	707 840	607 851	4 124 947	4 732 838	5 440 678	3 212 516	381 627	887 569	1 269 196	4 171 452	50 000 000

10

[C.]

A Statement showing the Exports from, and Home Consumption in, the United Kingdom of Great Britain and Ireland, of Cotton Yarns and Cotton Goods during the years 1858 to 1863.

Years.	Piece goods exported. Yards.	Piece goods exported. Value. £	Hosiery and small wares exported. Value. £	Twist and yarn exported. Pounds.	Twist and yarn exported. Value. £	Weight of goods and yarn exported, including loss in spinning. Lbs.	Total value of exports of cotton goods. £	Consumption of cotton goods in the United Kingdom. Weight. Lbs.	Equivalent to, in raw cotton. † Lbs.	Value. £	Total exports from and sales in the United Kingdom. £
1858	2 324 139 085	32 042 114	1 379 729	200 016 902	9 579 479	668 240 142	43 001 322	180 000 000	210 160 000	23 000 000	66 001 322
1859	2 562 545 476	37 038 538	1 705 575	192 206 643	9 458 112	684 300 189	48 202 225	185 000 000	215 160 000	23 500 000	71 702 225
1860	2 776 218 427	40 346 342	1 795 163	197 313 655	9 870 875	710 260 384	52 012 380	190 000 000	220 160 000	25 000 000	77 012 380
1861	2 563 459 007	36 124 685	1 455 043	177 848 353	9 292 761	701 170 311	46 872 489	190 000 000	225 160 000	28 000 000	74 872 489
1862	1 681 394 600	28 562 466	1 986 265	93 225 800	6 202 240	508 140 200	36 750 971	185 000 000	240 160 000‡	33 000 000	69 750 971
1863	1 706 572 858	37 541 485	1 832 525	74 642 146	8 019 954	544 984 572	47 443 964	180 000 000	250 160 000‡	48 000 000	95 443 964
	13 614 329 453	211 655 630	10 204 300	935 283 589	52 423 421	3 817 095 798	274 283 351	1 110 000 000	1 360 960 000	180 500 000	454 783 351

* No doubt undervalued, to evade duties.   See p. 7 and 8.   † Includes foreign goods.   ‡ Inferior cottons make less goods.

[D.]

A Statement showing the stocks of Raw Cotton in Spinners' hands, the Yarn-producing properties, and the Goods and Yarns in the hands of all classes, from the Spinners to the Retailers, in the United Kingdom on the 1st of January in each year; also the weight of the Cotton consumed, Yarns and Goods produced and exported, 1858 to 1863.

Years.	Stocks of raw cotton in spinners' hands, the yarn-producing properties, and the yarns and goods in the hands of all classes, from the spinners to the retailers, on the 1st of January of each year.		Cotton consumed by the mills in each year.	Yarns and goods produced in each year.	Yarns and goods exported in each year.	Excess of production over exports.	Excess of exports over production.	Net excess of production.
	Weight of cotton.	Yarn-producing properties.	Yarns and goods on hand.						
	Lbs.	Lbs.	Lbs.	* Lbs.	Lbs.	Lbs.	Lbs.	Lbs.	Lbs.
1858	100 960 000	85 900 000	400 000 000	895 600 000	795 000 000	610 741 000	184 259 000		
1859	110 000 000	55 000 000	415 000 000	966 600 000	859 250 000	633 871 000	225 379 000		
1860	120 000 000	105 000 000	465 000 000	1 073 600 000	973 650 000	748 722 000	224 928 000		
1861	150 000 000	135 000 000	510 000 000	997 400 000	846 500 000	684 886 000	161 614 000		
1862	100 000 000	80 000 000	460 000 000	444 500 000	365 000 000	410 000 000	-	45 000 000	
1863	50 000 000	35 000 000	270 000 000	553 260 000	400 000 000	390 000 000	10 000 000		
1864	20 000 000	15 000 000	100 000 000						
				4 930 960 000	4 239 400 000	3 478 220 000	806 180 000	45 000 000	761 180 000

* Includes the foreign cotton goods.

[E.]

Imports of Raw Cotton into the United Kingdom, as per Board-of-Trade Tables, during the years 1858 to 1863.

COUNTRIES.	1858. Cwts.	1859. Cwts.	1860. Cwts.	1861. Cwts.	1862. Cwts.	1863. Cwts.
Russia (Khiva and Bokhara),	-	213	57	4	9 199	632
Sweden,	34	830	-	8 894	1 696	252
*Danish West Indies, St. Croix, St. Thomas, &c.	1	9 461	-	1	11	1 338
*Holland,	2 393	4 004	1 655	8 307	6 337	1 047
Dutch Guiana,	1 120	427	682	326	546	807
*Belgium,	295	696	385	4 270	8 921	2 183
*France,	47 005	29 903	19 524	8 531	49 029	15 033
Portugal,	9	227	478	3 436	9 956	6 105
Spain and the Balearic Islands,	2	2 027	6	295	5 855	1 231
*Spanish Possessions, Cuba and Porto Rico,	56	-	3	114	27 230	34 473
Austrian Territories in Italy,	-	335	174	1 006	2 897	804
Greece,	-	-	-	415	2 005	3 080
Turkey in Europe and Asia,	101	3 551	66	598	38 797	108 876
Syria and Palestine,	-	-	44	35	2 415	1 418
Egypt,	341 360	336 313	392 447	365 108	526 897	835 289
*American States,	7 439 623	8 586 672	9 963 309	7 316 969	120 752	57 090
*Mexico,	-	-	-	-	27 960	172 196

Hayti and St. Domingo,	627	612	159	4 896	3 482	5 931
New Granada,	37	58	797	1 383	10 342	22 683
Venezuela,	625	–	1 213	–	111	742
Brazil,	166 231	200 705	154 347	154 378	208 384	201 814
Chili,		1	936		9	160
Peru,	2 484	2 305	2 571	3 585	2 252	275 503
China,			35		15 768	659
Western Coast of Africa,	2 116	1 816	2 039	1 399	3 438	3 400
Malta and Gozo,			100	2 473	2 165	63 807
*Bermudas,				90	5 024	222 469
*British West Indies, including Bahamas,	1 251	1 452	7 336	1 772	47 002	2 369
British Guiana,	2 033	3 836	2 046	2 480	2 671	
British East Indies,	1 185 023	1 717 240	1 822 689	3 205 004	3 505 844	3 678 757
Mauritius,	14 988	11 894	28 250	7 288	17 948	1 609
British Possessions, South Africa,	8 940	19 637	1 186	6 207	6 546	34 082
St. Helena,	17 953	1 211	–	819	2	6 352
Japan,						
Other countries,	891	10 855	16 532	22 955	6 842	16 301
Total,	9 235 198	10 946 331	12 419 096	11 223 078	4 678 333	5 978 422

*Chiefly American cottons re-exported. Many of the above named countries are not cotton growers. In some cases the produce was reshipped to England after the condemnation of the vessels, while in other instances, particularly during and since 1861, the high prices ruling at London and Liverpool attracted a portion of the Continental stocks of American cotton to those ports. A reverse current has now, however, set in; and the demand of the other nations of Europe for the raw material will require Great Britain to share her imports with them to a much greater extent than hitherto. They are all very bare of cotton and cotton goods, and are receiving but little cotton direct from the places of production. Nearly the whole of the supplies at sea and expected from other sources than the Mediterranean, are destined for England. The cotton that came to hand from St. Thomas, Cuba, Mexico, the Bermudas, and the Bahamas, with trifling exceptions, as well as a part of that credited to "other countries," was the growth of the Southern States of America—the places named being merely depots for blockade runners. The actual receipts from the Confederate States, direct and indirect, were—in 1862, 303,950 cwts. and in 1863, 551,284 cwts.; whereas the Board of Trade returns record only 120,752 cwts. for the former and 57,090 cwts. for the latter year. With the quantity of Southern cotton received on the Continent of Europe and in the Northern States of America in 1862 and 1863, the South, notwithstanding the partial blockade of her ports, has ranked as the second exporting country. Egypt stands third on the list. There has been no increase whatever in the cultivation of cotton in the British West Indies, Brazil, or in any sugar growing country.—G. McII.

[F.]

A Statement showing the approximate Annual Consumption of Raw Cotton by the Mills of Europe and America from 1836 to 1860.

YEARS.	Great Britain.	Russia, Germany, Holland, and Belgium.	France.	Spain and Portugal.	Adriatic States.	United States.	Sundries in the Mediterranean.	Total Consumption.
	Lbs.	Lbs.	Lbs.	Lbs.	Lbs.	Lbs.	Lbs.	Lbs.
1836,	350 000 000	57 000 000	118 000 000	—	28 000 000	86 000 000	—	639 000 000
1837,	359 000 000	58 000 000	121 000 000	—	32 000 000	86 000 000	—	656 000 000
1838,	435 000 000	61 000 000	133 000 000	—	26 000 000	92 000 000	—	747 000 000
1839,	362 000 000	48 000 000	110 000 000	—	26 000 000	103 000 000	—	649 000 000
1840,	473 000 000	72 000 000	157 000 000	—	28 000 000	111 000 000	—	841 000 000
1841,	422 000 000	65 000 000	154 000 000	—	29 000 000	115 000 000	—	785 000 000
1842,	462 000 000	78 000 000	163 000 000	—	38 000 000	105 000 000	—	846 000 000
1843,	531 000 000	82 000 000	152 000 000	—	44 000 000	131 000 000	—	940 000 000
1844,	543 000 000	86 000 000	146 000 000	—	26 000 000	143 000 000	—	944 000 000
1845,	597 000 000	96 000 000	158 000 000	—	38 000 000	158 000 000	—	1 047 000 000
1846,	604 000 000	97 000 000	159 000 000	—	39 000 000	175 000 000	—	1 074 000 000
1847,	425 000 000	105 000 000	196 000 000	—	31 000 000	175 000 000	—	862 000 000
1848,	591 000 000	112 000 000	127 000 000	—	29 000 000	209 000 000	—	1 068 000 000
1849,	627 000 000	160 000 000	186 000 000	—	47 000 000	205 000 000	—	1 225 000 000
1850,	584 000 000	133 000 000	142 000 000	29 000 000	45 000 000	188 000 000	—	1 121 000 000
1851,	648 000 000	118 000 000	149 000 000	34 000 000	45 000 000	158 000 000	23 000 000	1 175 000 000
1852,	745 000 000	172 000 000	199 000 000	44 000 000	55 000 000	237 000 000	29 000 000	1 481 000 000
1853,	765 000 000	185 000 000	194 000 000	42 000 000	45 000 000	265 000 000	38 000 000	1 534 000 000
1854,	780 000 000	190 000 000	201 000 000	43 000 000	45 000 000	243 000 000	37 000 000	1 539 000 000
1855,	840 000 000	200 000 000	190 000 000	45 000 000	39 000 000	235 000 000	69 000 000	1 618 000 000
1856,	910 000 000	260 000 000	210 000 000	48 000 000	39 000 000	266 000 000	56 000 000	1 789 000 000
1857,	826 000 000	214 000 000	165 000 000	60 000 000	56 000 000	317 000 000	40 000 000	1 678 000 000
1858,	906 000 000	230 000 000	175 000 000	67 000 000	60 000 000	239 000 000	60 000 000	1 737 000 000
1859,	976 000 000	240 000 000	210 000 000	70 000 000	60 000 000	371 000 000	70 000 000	1 997 000 000
1860,	1 100 000 000	264 000 000	231 000 000	70 000 000	60 000 000	400 000 000	80 000 000	2 205 000 000

The Cotton Spindles of Europe and America in 1860.

COUNTRIES.	Spindles.	Pounds.
Great Britain,	34 000 000	1 100 000 000
American States,	6 000 000	400 000 000
France,	6 000 000	260 000 000
Russia,	1 800 000	80 000 000
Austria,	2 000 000	70 000 000
Holland,	800 000	45 000 000
Switzerland,	1 500 000	40 000 000
Spain,	1 000 000	40 000 000
Belgium,	800 000	40 000 000
Bavaria,	700 000	35 000 000
Saxony,	600 000	30 000 000
Prussia,	500 000	25 000 000
Italy, Sardinia,	300 000	12 000 000
Mexico,	140 000	12 000 000
Wurtemburg,	200 000	10 000 000
Baden,	150 000	7 500 000
Norway, Sweden,	100 000	6 000 000
Naples, Sicily, Malta,	160 000	5 000 000
Hanover,	70 000	3 500 000
Oldenburgh,	60 000	3 000 000
Portugal,	30 000	1 500 000
	56 850 000	

For other purposes than manufacture in the
several countries, such as candle wicks,
stuffing furniture, etc. etc.   -   -   174 500 000

                                                        2 400 000 000

The countries that manufacture the coarsest
counts of yarn use the greatest number of pounds
of cotton to the spindle.

The raw cotton was contributed by the following countries:

Southern States,	-	2 078 577 600
India,	-	204 141 168
Brazil,	-	17 286 864
West Indies,	-	1 050 784
Other places,	-	98 943 584

                                                        2 400 000 000

THE COTTON TRADE OF GREAT BRITAIN IN 1860.

			BALES.	BALES.
Estimated stock of cotton, January 1, 1860,	-	-	–	469 520
Cotton imports in 1860—American,	-	-	2 438 236	
Cotton imports in 1860—Brazilian,	-	-	99 067	
Cotton imports in 1860—West Indian,	-	-	1 758	
Cotton imports in 1860—East Indian,	-	-	550 663	
Cotton imports in 1860—Egyptian,	-	-	113 963	
				3 203 687
				3 673 207
Cotton exports in 1860—American,	-	-	190 912	
Cotton exports in 1860—Brazilian,	-	-	50	
Cotton exports in 1860—East Indian,	-	-	289 238	
Cotton exports in 1860—other kinds,	-		803	
				481 003
				3 192 204
Estimated stock on January 1, 1861,	-	-	–	594 510
Number of cotton bales consumed,	-	-	–	2 597 694
Average pounds weight per bale—all kinds,	-	-	–	424
Pounds weight of cotton consumed,	-	-	–	1 101 422 256

The following particulars illustrate the importance of the cotton trade of Great Britain. In 1850 there were 21,000,000 spinning spindles and 250,000 power looms at work. On May 1st, 1856, there were 28,010,000 spindles and 298,847 power looms, or an increase of 7,000,000 spindles and 48,000 power looms in six years; the consumption of cotton having increased from 584,000,000 pounds to 910,000,000 pounds. Between 1856 and 1860 the cotton trade of Great Britain was increased from 28,000,000 to 34,000,000 spindles.

Amount paid for cotton by the spinners in 1860,	-	-	-		23,000,000
Wages,	-	-	-	-	-	15,000,000
Trade expenses and sundries,	-	-	-		15,000,000
Interest on capital,	-	-	-		8,000,000
Profits on spinning,	-	-	-		14,000,000
Profits on manufacturing,	-	-	-		5,000,090

£80,000,000

Value of goods exported,	-	-	-	53,000,000
Value of goods consumed in the United Kingdom at manufacturers' prices,	-	-	-	25,000,000
Value of goods on hand of the manufacture of 1860,	-			2,000,000

£80,000,000

There were also large quantities of cotton goods on hand, of the make of the several previous years.

[I.]

[From the New York Shipping List, of October 9, 1861.]

THE COTTON CROP OF THE SOUTHERN STATES.

Growth of 1860, *sent to market from September* 1, 1860, *to August* 31, 1861.

	BALES.		TOTAL.		
			1860.	1859.	1858.
LOUISIANA.					
Export from New Orleans:					
To foreign ports, -	1 783 673				
To coastwise ports, -	132 179				
Burnt at New Orleans, -	3 276				
Stock, September 1, 1861, -	10 118				
		1 929 246			
Deduct:					
Received from Mobile, -	48 270				
" " Montgomery, &c. -	11 551				
" " Florida, -	13 279				
" " Texas, -	30 613				
Stock, September 1, 1860, -	73 934				
		177 647			
			1 751 599	2 139 425	1 069 274
ALABAMA.					
Export from Mobile:					
To foreign ports, -	456 421				
To coastwise ports, -	127 574				
Manufactured in Mobile (estimated),	2 000				
Stock, September 1, 1861, -	2 481				
		588 476			
Deduct:					
Stock, September 1, 1860, -	41 682				
			546 794	843 012	704 406
TEXAS.					
Export from Galveston, &c.:					
To foreign ports, -	63 209				
To coastwise ports, -	84 254				
Stock, September 1, 1861, -	452				
		147 915			
Deduct:					
Stock, September 1, 1860, -	3 168				
			144 747	252 424	192 062
FLORIDA.					
Export f'm Apalachicola, St. Marks, &c.					
To foreign ports, -	28 073				
To coastwise ports, -	85 953				
Burnt at St. Marks, -	150				
Stock, September 1, 1861, -	7 860				
		122 036			
Deduct:					
Stock, September 1, 1860, -	864				
			121 172	192 724	173 484
GEORGIA.					
Export from Savannah:					
To foreign ports—Uplands, -	293 746				
To " Sea Islands, -	8 441				
To coastwise ports—Uplands, -	170 572				
To " Sea Islands, -	11 512				
Stock in Savannah, Sept. 1, 1861, -	4 102				
Stock in Augusta, &c. Aug. 1, 1861,	5 991				
		494 364			
Deduct:					
Received from Florida—Sea Islands, -	1 033				
" " " Uplands, -	6 188				
Stock in Savannah, Sept. 1, 1860, -	4 307				
Stock in Augusta, &c. Sept. 1, 1860, -	5 252				
		16 780			
11			477 584	525 219	475 788

	BALES.	TOTAL.		
		1860.	1859.	1858.
SOUTH CAROLINA.				
Exp't f'm Charleston and Georgetown :				
To foreign ports—Uplands,	199 345			
To " Sea Islands,	15 043			
To coastwise ports—Uplands,	121 663			
To " Sea Islands,	8 355			
Burnt at Charleston,	564			
Stock in Charleston, Sept. 1, 1861,	2 899			
		347 869		
Deduct:				
Received from Florida and Savannah—				
Uplands,	2 378			
Sea Islands,	255			
Stock in Charleston, Sept. 1, 1860,	8 897			
		11 530		
		336 339	510 109	480 653
NORTH CAROLINA.				
Export:				
To foreign ports,	195			
To coastwise ports,	56 100			
		—	56 295	41 194	37 482
VIRGINIA.				
Export:				
To foreign ports,	810			
To coastwise ports,	61 129			
Mannufactured (taken from the ports),	16 993			
Stock, September 1, 1861,	2 000			
		80 932		
Deduct:				
Stock, September 1, 1860,		2 800		
		78 132	56 987	33 011
TENNESSEE, ETC.				
Shipment from Memphis, Tenn.	369 857			
" " Nashville, "	16 471			
" " Columbus and Hickman, Ky.	5 500			
Stock at Memphis, Sept. 1, 1861,	1 671			
		393 499		
Deduct:				
Shipments to New Orleans,	196 366			
Manufactured on the Ohio, &c.	52 000			
Stock, September 1, 1860,	1 709			
		250 075		
		143 424	108 676	85 321
Total crop of the Southern States,	—	3 656 086	4 669 770	3 851 481

Decrease from crop of 1860,	· ·	1 013 684 bales,
Decrease from crop of 1859,	· ·	195 395 "
Increase over crop of 1858,	· ·	542 124 "
Increase over crop of 1857,	· ·	716 567 "

NOTE.—See page 29 for the exact particulars of the cotton crop of 1859—the largest ever grown—per census of 1860.

The average weight of American cotton bales was, in 1790, 200 pounds; in 1824, 300 pounds; in 1827, 336 pounds; in 1836, 370 pounds; in 1847, 400 pounds; in 1850, 410 pounds; in 1855, 420 pounds, and in 1860, 440 pounds. Mobile bales average 505 pounds; New Orleans, 460 pounds; Uplands, 400 pounds; Sea Islands, 250 to 325 pounds.

Comparative Crop Statement.

YEARS.	Bales.	YEARS.	Bales.
1824-5,	569 249	1843-4,	2 030 409
1825-6,	720 027	1844-5,	2 394 503
1826-7,	957 281	1845-6,	2 100 537
1827-8.	727 593	1846-7,	1 778 651
1828-9,	870 415	1847-8,	2 347 634
1829-30,	976 845	1848-9,	2 728 596
1830-1,	1 038 848	1849-50,	2 096 706
1831-2,	987 477	1850-1,	2 355 257
1832-3,	1 070 438	1851-2,	3 015 029
1833-4,	1 205 394	1852-3,	3 262 882
1834-5,	1 254 328	1853-4,	2 930 027
1835-6,	1 360 725	1854-5,	2 847 339
1836-7,	1 422 930	1855-6,	3 527 845
1837-8,	1 801 497	1856-7,	2 939 519
1838-9,	1 360 532	1857-8,	3 113 962
1839-40,	2 177 835	1858-9,	3 851 481
1840-1,	1 634 945	1859-60,	4 669 770
1841-2,	1 683 574	1860-1,	3 656 086
1842-3,	2 378 875		

Crop of Sea Island Cotton.

The crop of this staple for the past year* (included in the general statement) was as follows: Florida, —— bales; Georgia, —— bales; and South Carolina, —— bales; total, —— bales; against 46,649 bales in 1859-60; 47,592 in 1858-9; 40,566 in 1857-8; 45,314 in 1856-7; 44,512 in 1855-6; 40,841 in 1854-5; and 39,686 in 1853-4.

* This we are unable to give this year.—(See General Statement.)

Export to Foreign Ports from September 1, 1860, to August 31, 1861.

FROM	To Great Britain.	To France.	To North of Europe.	Other foreign ports.	TOTAL.
	Bales.	Bales.	Bales.	Bales.	Bales.
New Orleans, Louisiana,	1 159 348	388 925	122 042	113 358	1 783 673
Mobile, Alabama,	340 845	96 429	6 601	12 546	456 421
Galveston, Texas,	47 229	3 640	12 315	25	63 209
Florida,	27 140	–	933	–	28 073
Savannah, Georgia,	282 994	10 061	6 165	2 967	302 187
Charleston, South Carolina,	136 513	29 886	24 401	23 588	214 388
Virginia,	810	–	–	–	810
North Carolina,	144	–	–	51	195
New York,	158 415	49 122	35 197	5 315	248 049
Baltimore,	975	–	2 483	87	3 545
Philadelphia,	3 793	–	–	–	3 793
Boston,	17 019	–	6 113	93	23 225
Grand total,	2 175 225	578 063	216 250	158 030	3 127 568
Total last year,	2 669 432	589 587	295 072	220 082	3 774 173
Decrease,	494 207	11 524	78 822	62 052	646 605

Consumption.

		Bales.
Total crop of the Southern States, as before stated,	· ·	3 656 086

Add, stocks on hand at the commencement of year, Sept. 1, 1866:

In the Southern ports,	· · ·	142 613	
In the Northern ports,	· ·	85 095	
			227 708

		Makes a supply of	3 883 794

Deduct therefrom:

The export to foreign ports,	· ·	3 127 568	
Less, foreign included,	· ·	701	
			3 126 867
Stocks on hand Sept. 1, 1861—In Southern ports,		37 574	
" " " " In Northern ports,		45 613	
			83 187
Burnt at New Orleans, St. Marks, Charleston and Philadelphia,		4 390	
Manufactured in Virginia and Mobile,		18 993	
		23 383	
			3 233 437

Taken for home use North of Virginia,	· · ·	650 357
Taken for home use in Virginia and South and West of Virginia,	·	193 383
Total consumed in the United States (included burnt at the ports), 1860–61,		843 740

YEARS.		North Virginia.	Elsewhere.	TOTAL.
		Bales.	Bales.	Bales.
1847–8,	-	523 892	92 152	616 044
1848–9,	-	504 143	138 342	642 485
1849–50,	-	476 486	137 012	613 498
1850–1,	-	386 429	99 185	485 614
1851–2,	-	588 332	111 281	699 603
1852–3,	-	650 393	153 332	803 725
1853–4,	-	592 284	144 952	737 236
1854–5,	-	571 117	135 295	706 412
1855–6,	-	633 027	137 712	770 739
1856–7,	-	665 718	154 218	819 936
1857–8,	-	452 185	143 377	595 562
1858–9,	-	760 218	167 433	927 651
1859–60,	-	786 521	185 522	972 043
1860–1,	-	650 357	193 383	843 740

We give below our usual estimate of the amount of cotton consumed the past year in the States South and West of Virginia, and not included in the receipts at the ports. Thus:

	1854.	1855.	1856.	1857.	1858.	1859.	1860.	1861.
	Bales.	Bales.	Bales.	Bales.	Bales.	Bales.	Bales.	Bales.
North Carolina,	20 000	18 500	22 000	25 000	26 000	29 000	30 000	33 000
South Carolina,	12 000	10 500	15 000	17 000	18 000	20 000	21 000	24 000
Georgia,	23 000	20 500	25 000	23 000	24 000	26 000	28 000	32 000
Alabama,	6 000	5 500	6 500	5 000	8 000	10 000	11 000	12 000
Tennessee,	6 000	4 000	7 000	9 000	10 000	13 000	15 000	17 000
On the Ohio, &c.	38 000	26 000	42 000	38 000	39 000	45 000	49 000	52 000
Total to Sept. 1,	105 000	85 000	117 500	117 000	125 000	143 000	154 000	170 000

To which, if we add (for the past year) the stocks in the interior towns 1st September (say 6,200 bales), the quantity detained in the interior (say 25,000 bales), and that lost on its way to market (9,000 bales) to the crop as given above, received at the shipping ports, the aggregate will show, as near as may be, the amount raised in the Southern States the past season—say, in round numbers, 3,866,000 bales (after deducting 300 bales new crop received this year to 1st ult.), against

YEARS.			Bales.		YEARS.			Bales.
1849,	-	-	2 840 000		1855,	-	-	3 186 000
1850,		-	2 212 000		1856,	-	-	3 335 006
1851,	-	-	2 450 000		1857,	-	-	3 014 000
1852,	-	-	3 100 000		1858,	-	-	3 247 000
1853,	-	-	3 360 000		1859,	-	-	4 017 000
1854,	-	-	3 000 000		1860,	-	-	4 805 800

The quantity of new cotton received at the shipping ports to 1st September was—in

YEARS.			Bales.		YEARS.			Bales.
1834,	-	-	small.		1848,	-	-	3 000
1835,	-	-	3 424		1849,	-	-	575
1836,	-	-	9 702		1850,	-	-	255
1837,	-	-	no account.		1851,	-	-	3 200
1838,	-	-	no account.		1852,	-	-	5 125
1839,	-	-	no account.		1853,	-	-	6 716
1840,	-	-	30 000		1854,	-	-	1 890
1841,	-	-	32 000		1855,	-	-	26 079
1842,	-	-	3 000		1856,	-	-	1 800
1843,	-	-	300		1857,	-	-	100
1844,	-	-	7 500		1858,	-	-	8 031
1845,	-	-	7 500		1859,	-	-	12 369
1846,	-	-	200		1860,	-	-	51 600
1847,	-	-	1 121		1861,	-	-	300

We herewith present, about three weeks later than usual, our annual statement of the cotton crop of the Southern States. Owing to the unsettled state of the country and the absence of our usual mail facilities, our labor has been prosecuted with more difficulty, and less satisfaction to ourselves, than ever before, but we take pleasure in stating that owing to a combination of favorable circumstances we are, with a few unimportant exceptions, enabled to present a statement which, we believe, in all its leading items, *to approximate exactness,* and one which, for all practical purposes, may be considered reliable. Some of the minor details usually given in our statement are of necessity omitted, owing to the causes alluded to, and some others are less complete than we could wish, but we feel assured that the statement, as a whole, will be found very nearly correct. It is well known that, owing to the disturbed state of the Southern section of the country, the commerce in cotton was hurried to a close some two months or more earlier than usual, and the results now given were more or less correctly known a month or two ago. It will be well, however, to observe here that our former (weekly) tables included as receipts all the shipments from Memphis; but to arrive at the commercial crop of the country, we have as usual deducted the amount consumed on the Ohio, &c., estimated by good judges at 52,000 bales, and on this account the aggregate crop will now appear less than was previously supposed it would be. The statement, however, must speak for itself; it is the best we could make, considering the serious embarrassments under which we have labored.

An error in the Savannah statement last year (an excess of 6,000 bales in the coastwise shipments of Sea Island) is now corrected in the comparisons of crop, consumption, &c., which appear that much less than in our last year's account.

It may be well to observe that the preceding statement of the crop is that of the Southern States as a whole, *and does not purport to be the crops of the States,* though the shipments, stocks, &c. are necessarily arranged under the different leading shipping ports or States, as the case may be.

The Cotton Trade at its Height—Import, Consumption and Stock in Europe.

	S. States.	Brazil.	W. Ind.	E. Ind.	Egypt.	Total.
				1860.		
	Bales.	Bales.	Bales.	Bales.	Bales.	Bales.
Stock 1st January, -	374 000	33 000	4 000	144 000	16 000	571 000
Import to 31st December:						
Great Britain, -	2 582 000	103 000	10 000	563 000	110 000	3 368 000
France, -	610 000	2 000	26 000	12 000	35 000	685 000
· Holland, -	70 000	–	3 000	63 000	–	136 000
Belgium, -	35 000	–	1 000	25 000	–	61 000
Germany, -	183 000	–	7 000	111 000	–	301 000
Trieste, -	36 000	–	–	36 000	12 000	84 000
Genoa,	58 000	–	–	19 000	1 000	78 000
Spain, -	101 000	4 000	–	–	–	105 000
	3 675 000	109 000	47 000	829 000	158 000	4 818 000
*Deduct intermediate shipments,	124 000	3 000	–	256 000	–	383 000
	3 551 000	106 000	47 000	573 000	158 000	4 435 000
Add stock from above, -	374 000	33 000	4 000	144 000	16 000	571 000
Total supply, -	3 925 000	139 000	51 000	717 000	174 000	5 006 000
Deduct stock 31st December,	541 000	14 000	5 000	193 000	29 000	782 000
Total deliveries, -	3 384 000	125 000	46 000	524 000	145 000	4 224 000
Deliveries:						
In Great Britain, -	2 242 000	113 000	6 000	176 000	96 000	2 633 000
France, -	551 000	3 000	26 000	8 000	33 000	621 000
Holland, -	67 000	–	4 000	46 000	–	117 000
Belgium, -	34 000	–	1 000	29 000	–	64 000
Germany, -	177 000	–	9 000	121 000	–	307 000
Trieste, -	29 000	–	–	37 000	11 000	77 000
Genoa, -	54 000	–	–	17 000	1 000	72 000
Spain, -	103 000	3 000	–	–	–	106 000
†Surplus of export—Great Brit.	127 000	6 000	–	90 000	4 000	227 000
Total deliveries, -	3 384 000	125 000	46 000	524 000	145 000	4 224 000
Total deliveries in 1859, -	2 880 000	124 000	32 000	442 000	173 000	3 651 000
Stock 31st Dec. 1860-61-62:						
Great Britain, -	395 000	12 000	4 000	157 000	27 000	595 000
France, -	97 000	–	–	6 000	2 000	105 000
Holland, -	5 000	–	–	17 000	–	22 000
Belgium, -	2 000	–	–	–	–	2 000
Germany, -	11 000	–	1 000	8 000	–	20 000
Trieste, -	8 000	–	–	2 000	–	10 000
Genoa, -	5 000	–	–	3 000	–	8 000
Spain, -	18 000	2 000	–	–	–	20 000
	541 000	14 000	5 000	193 000	29 000	782 000
Stock 31st Dec. 1857-58-59,	311 000	39 000	11 000	239 000	26 000	626 000

Of the exports, those marked (*) were to France, Holland, Belgium, Trieste, Genoa and Spain, and are comprised in the imports to those places; and those marked (†) were to the Baltic, &c.

The Cotton Trade, &c.—Continued.

	1861.					
	S. States.	Brazil.	W. Ind.	E. Ind.	Egypt.	Total.
	Bales.	Bales.	Bales.	Bales.	Bales.	Bales.
Stock in January,	541 000	14 000	5 000	193 000	29 000	782 000
Import to 31st December:						
Great Britain,	1 842 000	99 000	11 000	986 000	97 000	3 035 000
France,	521 000	1 000	22 000	19 000	41 000	604 000
Holland,	98 000	–	–	75 000	–	173 000
Belgium,	27 000	–	–	21 000	–	48 000
Germany,	153 000	–	4 000	166 000	–	323 000
Trieste,	9 000	–	–	44 000	11 000	64 000
Genoa,	30 000	–	–	15 000	–	45 000
Spain,	82 000	3 000	–	8 000	15 000	108 000
	2 762 000	103 000	37 000	1 334 000	164 000	4 400 000
*Deduct intermediate shipments,	142 000	1 000	–	335 000	1 000	479 000
	2 620 000	102 000	37 000	999 000	163 000	3 921 000
Add stock from above,	541 000	14 000	5 000	193 000	29 000	782 000
Total supply,	3 161 000	116 000	42 000	1 192 000	192 000	4 703 000
Deduct stock 31st December,	429 000	28 000	2 000	398 000	15 000	872 000
Total deliveries,	2 732 000	88 000	40 000	794 000	177 000	3 831 000
Deliveries:						
In Great Britain,	1 691 000	82 000	14 000	355 000	111 000	2 253 000
France,	494 000	1 000	22 000	19 000	42 000	578 000
Holland,	96 000	–	–	89 000	–	185 000
Belgium,	28 000	–	–	21 000	–	49 000
Germany,	160 000	–	3 000	168 000	–	331 000
Trieste,	16 000	–	–	45 000	10 000	71 000
Genoa,	34 000	–	–	16 000	–	50 000
Spain,	92 000	4 000	–	2 000	13 000	111 000
†Surplus of export—Great Brit.	121 000	1 000	1 000	79 000	1 000	203 000
Total deliveries,	2 732 000	88 000	40 000	794 000	177 000	3 831 000
Total deliveries in 1860,	3 384 000	125 000	46 000	524 000	145 000	4 224 000
Stock 31st Dec. 1860-61-62:						
Great Britain,	283 000	27 000	1 000	378 000	10 000	699 000
France,	124 000	–	–	6 000	1 000	131 000
Holland,	7 000	–	–	3 000	–	10 000
Belgium,	1 000	–	–	–	–	1 000
Germany,	4 000	–	1 000	6 000	–	11 000
Trieste,	1 000	–	–	1 000	2 000	4 000
Genoa,	1 000	–	–	2 000	–	3 000
Spain,	8 000	1 000	–	2 000	2 000	13 000
	429 000	28 000	2 000	398 000	15 000	872 000
Stock 31st Dec. 1857-58-59,	412 000	27 000	6 000	72 000	40 000	557 000

Of the exports, those marked (*) were to France, Holland, Belgium, Trieste, Genoa and Spain, and are comprised in the imports to those places; and those marked (†) were to the Baltic, &c.

www.ingramcontent.com/pod-product-compliance
Lightning Source LLC
Chambersburg PA
CBHW021421090426
42742CB00009B/1209